FATHER OF
FOO

FATHER OF FOOTBALL

THE STORY OF SIR MATT BUSBY

FOREWORD BY BOBBY CHARLTON

DAVID MILLER

PAVILION

This edition published in 1994 by
PAVILION BOOKS LIMITED
26 Upper Ground, London SE1 9PD

First published in paperback in 1995

First published in 1971

A CIP catalogue record for this book is available from the
British Library

ISBN 1 85793 796 1

Printed and bound in Great Britain
by Cox & Wyman

2 4 6 8 10 9 7 5 3 1

Typeset in Sabon

This book may be ordered by post direct from the publisher.
Please contact the Marketing Department.
But try your bookshop first.

ACKNOWLEDGEMENTS

I would like to express my grateful thanks to the many people who at the time gave valuable assistance: in particular to David Meek and Michael Nimmo who read the manuscript and made numerous helpful suggestions, as did Frank Taylor, to whom I was also indebted for permission to draw upon material from his book *The Day a Team Died*; to the late Jimmy Murphy, Bobby Charlton, Bill Foulkes and all the other Manchester United players and officials who freely gave their time in recounting events; to Ernest Hecht of *Souvenir Press* for permission to draw upon material from *My Story* by Matt Busby (1957) and the *International Football Book*; to *The Times, Observer, Daily Telegraph, Sunday Telegraph, The F.A. News* and *Goal* magazine for permission to reproduce various items.

My sincere appreciation was due to Sir Matt Busby, who gave me some of his valuable time and kindly read the finished proofs. Sir Matt had declined personally to collaborate in the manuscript, as he had his autobiography pending.

D.M.

CONTENTS

FOREWORD

We were all proud of Matt Busby, and considered it a privilege to have played under his management. His achievements were enormous: he was a pioneer in Europe with Manchester United, against the wishes of the Football League; he created the 'Babes', 16-year-olds thrown in with men, at a time when that was unprecedented; he wanted the fans to have something to be proud of, making his teams thrill them with their dashing approach; he offered a great opportunity to show progress in stadium design and comfort for the fans, after the Old Trafford ground had been bombed during the war.

He changed completely the commercial side of the game: a development association to improve training facilities away from Old Trafford at The Cliff; indoor playing areas; the first floodlights on a training ground. All of these innovations were his. After seeing Real Madrid for the first time, he returned to tell us that they were playing a different game on the continent, that we had to become part of the wider football world. He set records in the transfer market: Tommy Taylor, Albert Quixall, Harry Gregg.

Yet while all this was going on, he had time to talk and laugh with all those he was leading. All were equal in his book. The players were his beloved boys, so the Munich crash was a nightmare come true. In the Rechts der Isar Hospital, they mended him and some of his flock. On his return, he took charge again from his great friend and coach Jimmy Murphy, who had been tireless in his efforts to keep the club afloat by bringing in new players to supplement the now inexperienced squad.

The Boss said it would take five years to bring the club back to anything like its former self, and it was that almost to the day when Manchester United won the F.A. Cup in 1963. The way he planned and eventually succeeded in bringing the highest success back to the club is well documented in these pages, and how, through his indestructible personality, he overcame physical and emotional injury.

He gave people in Manchester, in particular, a way of life, and has made Manchester United a favourite football club throughout the world, generating supporters' clubs everywhere. The fans love the club and they loved Sir Matt. People who worked with him admired and respected him, if not always agreeing with his decisions.

I suppose most people don't usually have affection for a football manager, although they may have allegiance. There is no automatic promotion when managers succeed, and this sometimes encourages them to appear rather mercenary. This is what many nowadays feel about managers, but the Old Man was different—unique. He was promoted to the board, and then became president, the position he held when he died. His achievements are legend, but I think the fact that he was truly loved by football people would have gratified him the most.

David Miller knew him through good and bad times, and I am sure you will enjoy reading his story of football's biggest man.

SIR BOBBY CHARLTON CBE

PREFACE

For a quarter of a century, Matt Busby and the teams he led to unprecedented triumphs were admired wherever they went. At times there was controversy, of course, but they never lost sight of the fact that football was a game to be enjoyed by both those who played and those who watched. It was a philosophy which is often forgotten in the way the game is played today. Matt Busby's teams, the excellence of those he gathered around him, fired the imagination of people all over the globe; they were the heroes of millions of boys, my son among them in the sixties, some of whom probably could not tell you where Manchester was on the map.

Busby inspired his teams to play in a way that demanded admiration; at their best, they were not bound by the conventions of the moment, for their style was a blend of many individuals, a formula which crossed the bridge between artisan and artist. Football, it has been said, is a combination of war, chess and ballet. Manchester United under Busby always possessed all three to a degree, but to each they also gave a showmanship, the touch of show-biz which made them, and him, unique in their time. So different were they from the majority of contemporary teams throughout the late forties, fifties, and sixties that they generated an envy that at times became unbearable among the rivals who experienced it. That era of Charlton, Law and Best became part of everyday language, like Gilbert and Sullivan or Marks and Spencer. They became a part of us. Those who died at Munich had not had time to enter such a state of national familiarity, for their names were mostly new and young, their premature fame galloping ahead of them. Yet because they were so young, Edwards and Coleman, Jones, Scanlan and Pegg, and the slightly older Taylor and Byrne, there was a national affection for them that transcended sport; and it was these boys who died before their prime, nurtured and matured by Busby beyond their years, who really established the legend that became imperishable.

'For me, what was unique about that first team I played with [before Munich] was the blend,' Bobby Charlton says. 'When we were really going the balance was perfect. Matt Busby never really did a lot on the field at training, except join in. Leading up to the accident, I honestly believe there was little you could teach that team. My first real glimpse of Matt was at youth team cup tie. He was a distant, lofty figure. There was a bit of a hush in the dressing room, wondering what he would say. "Get to the ball first" was about the extent of it, but we sat there and thought: Fantastic! What a great man! He had this aura, a strange kind of ability to inspire you to play above yourself without actually saying much.'

Of course Matt Busby was less than perfect. He had flaws, some of which are discussed in this book which was first published 24 years ago at the moment of his initial retirement, from which for a brief time he returned to the game. It is easy to see, or to say, with hindsight that Busby should not have remained there at the head of the institution he had created, confusing the picture, initially, for those whose job it was to try to emulate him. Yet what was he to do? Where was he to go? We should remember and understand what kind of man he was and where he came from. He was a miner's son who, besides possessing an unusual conception of what the game of football could and should be, set about creating within the game those things that had been absent from his childhood: security, reliability, warmth, unity. Temperamentally, never mind materially, it would have been a nonsense, a contradiction, for him to have turned his back upon the house that he had built around him. He never believed, I am sure, that by staying he might temporarily undermine his own creation, though maybe to some extent that is what he inadvertently did.

Nor should Busby be blamed if, in his later allegiance with the Manchester United chairman Louis Edwards, he was a partner to a regime in which some of the principles, off the field, for which Manchester United had once stood, now became blurred or ignored. Busby had always had the view that directors should be the servants of the club, that they were there to support the football, not to control or direct it; and in Louis Edwards, Busby no doubt felt that he found a potential chairman who was *manageable*. While Busby himself had been blessed with an instinctive sense of leadership and fairness, of treating Irene and Joan, the ladies who did the laundry at Old Trafford, on a par with the most famous of his players, and while all his life he had the most dignified bearing, it was not in his nature or his training to head-hunt the ideal employer. No doubt he expected from Louis Edwards the same standards which in himself he took for granted, and if over a period of years Edwards partially allowed Manchester United to drift into becoming just another football club, that is not a responsibility which can be laid at Busby's door. Indeed, the legacy that Busby gave to Manchester United has survived the subterraneous erosion that occurred during some of the uncertain years of the seventies and eighties. The mark that Busby made on the game would survive the passing indiscretions of others, and this much was apparent at the time he died in January, 1994. The essential goodness that Busby brought to football will continue to be recognised for many years, even by those young enough to be his grandsons and upon whom he had no professional influence. It is recognised by Bryan Robson, one of the most resolute of players in Manchester United's post-war history. The only advice given to Robson by the Grand Old Man, in retirement, was always: 'Have fun . . . there's no other point in playing.' If only there were more in the game nowadays who understood that.

In a distinctive way, Matt Busby became part of the soul of Manchester, and this was something that continued to be felt by people throughout the city until the end of his life. Born on May 26, 1909, he died peacefully, aged 84, on January 20, 1994. On the day of his funeral, as the cortège behind the coffin wound its way through Manchester streets *en route* to the Southern Cemetery, people lined the pavement two- and three-deep. The elderly came to their front door to watch, or stood gazing from bedroom windows.

As the grey skies wept, so did grown men and women for whom Sir Matt *was* Manchester. Men removed their hats in the driving rain, tradesmen stood beside their stationary vans in the middle of the road, middle-aged mothers held gloved hands over their mouths to stifle their sorrow, schoolchildren, many of whom would never have seen him in the flesh but for whom his name is legendary, lined the roads, some with their hands held in prayer. 'The difference between this and other funerals,' Paddy Crerand, a Scotland wing-half so similar in mould to the elegant Busby, reflected afterwards outside St. John's Roman Catholic Church in Chorlton, 'is that everything people are saying today they said when Matt was alive. So often it's just being polite.'

Harry Gregg, who had helped pull Busby's broken body from the crashed plane at Munich, was as near to tears as anyone. 'He wasn't a talker unless you got him privately,' Gregg said. 'After Munich, he said that it wasn't his own pain that hurt him [they had to re-set his fractured foot without anaesthetic because of his punctured lung] but the sight of one of his own team mentally broken, and the grief of not being able to confirm to other players that Duncan Edwards or Tommy Taylor had gone.' Brian Kidd, whose goals at Wembley helped Busby achieve his ambition—the winning of the European Cup against Benfica in 1968—and who now coaches Old Trafford youngsters, appreciates what Busby taught him about people as much as what he learned about football. 'He never undermined any-one's self-respect,' Kidd says. 'When you were down, he lifted you with an arm round your shoulder. If you were cocky, he cautioned you. He gave you a conscience in your actions.'

As Busby went, dressed in his club blazer and tie, to lie alongside his beloved wife Jean, all along the way there was mute evidence of the admiration, gratitude and affection that he generated during nearly a half a century. By the time their hero—for truly he was a hero—paused at the Old Trafford stadium, the people were standing ten-deep. The affection did not end there. There were almost 9,000 present a month later for the memorial service held at Old Trafford: a larger gathering of people than there had been at all but six matches the previous day in three divisions of the Endsleigh League. I relate this not to dwell morbidly on Busby's death, but as evidence of the impact he still carried a quarter of a century after he had ceased to be in charge. Cliff Morgan, the former Welsh international rugby player who made the memorial address, recalled the benign, understanding eyes of the Grand Old Man, which gaze at Morgan every morning from the portrait at his home painted by Harold Riley, one of Busby's closest friends. 'They tell all there is to know about the man, his indestructibility and his goodness,' Morgan reflected. Morgan had a direct line of contact with Busby through Jimmy Murphy, a fellow fervent Welshman and Busby's partner and confidant at Old Trafford, where his avuncular coaching fashioned the rare talent of raw boys into competitive refinement, allowing them to retain their distant awe of Busby. 'From the same Rhondda coal tip,' Murphy said, typically, when first introducing Morgan to Busby. 'When you met him,' Morgan said, speaking for everyone who had ever had the good fortune to do so, 'he gave you the feeling you were the only one he wanted to see. . . . He understood the beauty of the game, of Charlton, Law and Best, of Kanchelskis and Cantona. He was sustained by an unshakeable belief in his God. What a legacy he has left in this club. He inspired in the players a sense of nationhood, a pride and style. Perhaps he didn't invent football, but he sewed a special, beautiful piece of material into football's robes of state.' There was a special warmth that day in the reception given to Charlie Mitten, Charlton, Gregg, and Dennis Law. This was a family reunion. Here was a view of ordinary Britain, as portrayed by a page from Priestley or a canvas by Lowry. Mancunians were quietly paying tribute to someone particularly loved in our twentieth-century social history. The reasons are contained in this story I first attempted to tell back in 1970 . . .

—1—
REVOLUTIONARY

Liverpool in 1938—a sprawl of smoke-smelly cobbled streets and anonymous slate-grey little houses, full of warmth inside but intimidating to the stranger without. Not a city in which to be alone. A time when to have a job, any job, was then, as now, still as much a matter of dignity as security. There was still a fence, and you could be in no doubt on which side of it you were. Promotion and position were to be sought not for satisfaction but exploitation: if Jack wasn't all right, no one was much likely to notice.

At about nine-thirty every morning a man boarded the tram just to the east side of the Mersey Tunnel. As often as not, already sitting there was someone noticeable for his tidy, dapper appearance: fawn overcoat, trilby, pipe, newspaper—a bank manager, perhaps, or the man from the Pru'. It was, in fact, Matthew Busby, professional footballer, on his way to the Liverpool Football Club ground at Anfield, together with his colleague Cliff Lloyd; each later to become outstanding administrators within the game. Their lives subsequently moved in different directions, but their aims were in many ways identical—to raise the status of an already world-wide game.

Then, as later, Matt Busby was ahead of his time. To a game fostered in the middle of the nineteenth century by those from the famous public schools, but now considered by most as the preserve of the proletariat, Busby unerringly brought dignity, elegance and style, perhaps above all a self-respect for the individual. Over 20 years later his unprecedented achievements as a manager and Lloyd's quieter diligence as Secretary of the Professional Footballers'

Association were to help force the professionals' right to basic freedoms of employment into the High Court.

Having become the most respected, almost revered, figure in the game, having experienced heaven and hell yet with magnification rather than distortion of his personality, he was voted, in a Gallup-Poll, on February 3, 1969, the seventh most admired man in Britain. He had been knighted, the previous summer, not just because the club he managed, Manchester United, had become the first English club to win the coveted European Cup, but because in 40 years' professional service to the game he had made a unique contribution to human relationships. This Catholic Scot, son of a miner, had proved himself, in every sense, a singular man.

Without ostentation he was the leader or instigator in almost every important development in the game. The list is long, but probably most influential of all was his realisation that to build a successful club, the most expedient and permanent way was to seek out and train from scratch the best schoolboys in the country, moulding in them not only his own tactics but his ideals, fashioning them for fame. He was one of the first to leave the manager's desk and exchange his office suit for a track-suit, keen to establish that bond with his players which was previously almost unknown. Most managers were little more than foreman draughtsmen, seeing their players once or twice a week. Realising not so much the value as the necessity of coaching, Busby surrounded himself with skilled men of character, to ensure consistency and continuity throughout every level of the club, which won the Football Association Youth Cup five times in a row.

He was the first to establish indisputably that he and not the directors was in control of all team affairs, at a time when directors were all-powerful and to stand up to them was unprecedented. In the gentlest way, like a hospital matron, he had dominated his board, even to the extent of persuading the rest of the directors to oppose the chairman over the election of a new member. His former chairman, the late Harold Hardman, one of the most benevolent of men, once said when asked how things were done at Old Trafford, home of the club: 'Matt will seek the board's advice, ponder over it, and then go away and do precisely what he wants to.'

With his deep-rooted sense of fair play, Busby shocked other clubs of the Football League—and even inadvertently caused change in legislation to prevent such 'abuse'—by paying benefits to players sometimes short of the prescribed time, and to those who were still almost boys but had the regulation amount of service. If a 17-year-old was promoted to the first team he was paid first-team wages: this in the days when there was a rigorous maximum wage for all clubs, allegedly for the 'good' of the game but in fact for no other purpose than to help the small clubs survive. Busby also constantly pressed for a rationalisation of this anomaly, yet he was quick to check any youngster in a financial hurry. Wilf McGuinness, who succeeded Busby as team manager in 1969, remembers when, as a boy of 18 just promoted to the first team, he went to 'The Boss', as Busby was known throughout the club, to say that he thought two players were wrongly getting more than he was, though they were the same age. With that paternal and unanswerable firmness Busby restrained him. 'Son, don't go chasing money. If you're good enough, you'll get it; the same with publicity, anything.' Patience has not been the least of his own virtues.

Realising the potential in finance and prestige of the European Cup, not only to his own club but to the English game, he turned his back in 1956 on the recommendation of the conservative and myopic Football League management committee not to compete, and entered his team for the competition which was to bring him his greatest tragedy and triumph. Always his eye was on the advancement and development of the team, always he was looking for fresh experience. 'Money in the bank is no use to a football team,' he said. 'You have to put your money on the field where the public can see it.' Though planning to produce his own players, he was never slow to go for outstanding players on the transfer market who he thought would enhance the club. One of these was Albert Quixall, an England international at 19, whom he bought from Sheffield Wednesday in 1958 for the then record fee of £45,000. Quixall later wrote: 'Matt is burning to win the European Cup. But much more important, he wants to win it gloriously. He wants the sort of team which will make everybody in Britain rejoice.'

Above all, he wanted his players to enjoy themselves, to find fun in the game. Always he had learned the lesson of his experience. Remembering the unhappiness and uncertainty of his early days as a player, he made sure as a manager that within his club there was harmony, that none should harbour resentment. It is hard to believe, so embracing was his sense of fairness to all, from greatest star to humble ground-staff boy. It is difficult, if not impossible, to find a player who will speak ill of him. In the late sixties I met three of his former players, then all with the same club—Albert Kinsey, Ian Moir and David Gaskell. All three had gone to Old Trafford as boys, buoyant with the ambitions which we all have at that age, especially when even to be signed on by the club is an acknowledgement of potential. Yet none of these three, then playing in relative obscurity with Wrexham, bore the slightest grudge or resentment, or felt that in being discarded they had been treated unjustly. There was only admiration.

In tactics, Busby was always at the forefront. His most famous team of all, from 1955 to 1958, many of whom perished in the Munich air crash, were using a 4–2–4 formation two years before the World Champions, Brazil, made it fashionable. This same team pioneered the strategy of playing defensively on the away leg of two-leg matches. Having always possessed forwards of extraordinary flair, he allowed them to attack uninhibitedly, which gained his teams a reputation for being defensively poor, yet the record shows this to be false. Long before the Dutch 'total football' of the seventies he had emphasised the importance of the all-round player rather than the specialist. Of the famous Hungarians of the 1950s, he considered Bozsik, their wing-half with incomparable perception, to be the essence of the team, rather than Puskas, the deadly goal-scorer; while he regarded Di Stefano, the Argentinian who helped Real Madrid of Spain to win the European Cup the first five times, as the most complete and, therefore, the greatest player he had ever seen.

Towards the end of the sixties a phrase that became increasingly used among the game's tacticians was 'work-rate', a conception of all-round effort from every player at every moment of a match which was given impetus by England's victory in the 1966 World Cup. Yet in 1960 Busby had stated: 'I look forward to the day when we place a premium on ability to read the game and play it mentally without the ball, and on adaptability, when all forwards can play in all positions', a view anticipating Alf Ramsey and Martin Peters in 1966. In a few years every manager, journalist and television commentator was repeatedly talking of 'running off the ball'. This, and versatility, was exemplified to perfection in the spring of 1968 when Bill Foulkes, a full-back, survivor of Munich and an unsung hero of 30 European Cup-ties, scored the goal which sank Real Madrid and put Manchester United in the final, in which they beat Benfica. Anticipating a run up the wing by George Best, by now the brightest star in the Manchester firmament, Foulkes caught Madrid on the hop and was there in the goal-mouth when Best finally turned the ball back to him.

When Manchester United had beaten Benfica, giving Busby his ultimate reward, his record of unparalleled achievement since he took charge of the club in 1945 stood as follows:

League Champions five times: 1952, 1956, 1957, 1965, 1967.
Runners-up seven times: 1947, 1948, 1949, 1951, 1959, 1964, 1968.
F.A. Cup winners twice: 1948, 1963
Runners-up twice: 1957, 1958
Semi-finalists five times: 1949, 1962, 1964, 1965, 1966 (later 1970).
European Cup winners: 1968.
Semi-finalists three times: 1957, 1958, 1966 (later 1969).
Fairs Cup semi-finalists: 1965.
F.A. Youth Cup winners six times: 1953, 1954, 1955, 1956, 1957, 1964.

Yet in spite of this mammoth testimony to his leadership he retained an uncanny equanimity in victory and defeat; in this aspect of the game, too, demonstrating a philosophy which many managers, hustling for success, could do well to emulate. Stan Cullis, the Wolves manager, said: 'He's a difficult bloke to read after a game.

You can't tell whether he's been on the winning or losing side. He seems able to absorb an extraordinary amount of defeat.' In this respect he set down his attitude concisely in his speech on the occasion of being made a Freeman of Manchester in November 1967, an attitude all but abandoned over the next 25 years. He said:

'I won't deny that it is pleasant to succeed in what you strive to do, but winning matches at all costs is not the test of true achievement. There is nothing wrong in trying to win, so long as you don't set the prize above the game. There is no dishonour in defeat, so long as you play to the limit of your strength and skill. What matters above all is that the game should be played in the right spirit, with the utmost resource of skill and courage, with fair play and no favour, with every man playing as a member of a team, the result accepted without bitterness or conceit.

'There are two other aspects of the game that have always impressed me. I love its drama, its smooth playing skill—and its great occasions, for example the Cup Final in the great arena at Wembley. I feel a sense of romance, wonder and mystery, a sense of poetry. On such occasions the game is larger than life.'

The then Prime Minister, Harold Wilson, speaking at a party afterwards, said: 'Matt Busby is the symbol of everything that is best in our great national game.' Yet what did the man himself expect of his players? As you would suppose, he was as much concerned with the inner fibre of the player as with any dexterity of the feet. Once, when asked what qualities made a Manchester United player, he replied: 'Skill, fitness and character—and the most important of these is character.' Today, we wonder sometimes if Alex Ferguson understands this principle. It has been said that Busby was a manager only of good players, that he would have laboured if he had had to make do with the lesser material of other clubs. But this was to overlook his ability to spot which were the good and which the bad, and to let the bad go before they became disillusioned; though Johnny Carey, captain of the team with which Busby first won the F.A. Cup in 1948, was of the opinion that 'Matt's loyalty to players is such that sometimes he has given it to those who were not worthy of it'. Conversely, Busby somehow had the ability to insult players when necessary without hurting their feelings, and the knack, as another manager complains, 'of having three players on £10,000 a year without any problems from those on £6,000, while we have trouble from those on £4,000 if we have one on £5,000.'

Simply, his ability to keep his players happy lay in their willingness to trust him. George Best said that what impressed him most 'was The Boss's honesty'—and added, somewhat ruefully in the light of escapades that found him caught out: 'He seems to know everything that's going on in Manchester.' Bobby Charlton, a player respected throughout the world as much for his sportsmanship as his remarkable swerve and shooting power, recalled that as a youngster 'you always knew that he knew more than you did, and if ever you thought to yourself "I wonder why he doesn't do so-and-so" you'd find that a few days later it had happened. What was reassuring was that his door was always open to you.'

They say in show business that one should never trample on anyone on the way up because you are sure to meet them on the way down. This is very true of football management, and was perceived by Busby. So many managers have modelled themselves on him, come to him for advice, attempted to emulate his methods—Don Revie, Joe Mercer, Tommy Docherty, and many others.

One of the things Busby learned on his visits to Real Madrid was the value of an unfailingly high standard of hospitality and courtesy to other clubs and managers, and whatever his own problems may have been at that moment, he found time for his guests. Revie recalled that in the mid-1960s, just after Leeds had been promoted from the Second Division, they beat Manchester at Old Trafford, 1–0. 'But Matt showed no signs of disappointment. His first concern was that we should feel at home, that our players should have sandwiches and beer or whatever they wanted. You would never have supposed that he had just lost. Another time, when we went out of the Cup to Everton in the semi-final at Old Trafford, he came up afterwards, put his arm round my shoulder and took me off to his room for a double brandy, saying: "I know how it feels, it's happened to us five times, but don't let your chin drop, it'll come."' The next season Leeds won the League Championship.

The courtesy was extended to all alike. When in my early days as a correspondent I went to Old Trafford for a memorable Charity Shield match against Manchester City, I had not then met Matt, but, without any question, there was a complimentary ticket for my wife and a pass for her to the directors' lounge after the match. Contrast this with the club where some of the 1966 World Cup matches were played, and the commissionaire refused entry to the manager of the Hungarian team, even when told who he was, because he had no ticket. Tommy Cavanagh, when assistant manager at Nottingham Forest, told the story of when he was manager of Brentford and called at Old Trafford hoping to buy not some £80,000 player but one for £1,000—in three instalments! He was greeted as if from Santos or Internazionale, offered brandy and cigars, neither of which he touched, and came away feeling the grandest man in the game—but without the player.

A characteristic of all great men in the field is attention to detail. Nothing was too small for Busby—half a pound of tea for Johnny Carey's sister in Northern Ireland just after the war when rationing was still on, a present for George Best's young brother, a baby-sitter for a player whose wife was ill, flowers for the wife of a manager from whom he had just bought a player. Not, let the cynics note, to get what he wanted, but *after* he had got it.

Nor was he too big to admit his own mistakes. Jack Crompton, Manchester United's trainer, remembers the time when Busby agreed to let some of the younger players have Saturday morning off training. Then on Friday, when Crompton had already told them and they were away from Old Trafford, training at the Y.M.C.A. ground at Fallowfield, Busby changed his mind. So he got into his car and drove down to Fallowfield himself, to explain to the boys that it was his fault, not Crompton's.

A common failing of the British, laughed at by Americans, is our failure to remember people's names. Avoiding this is more important, in some ways, with people who are not of any consequence in your life, because you do not then give an impression of ignoring them. Noël Coward once said to a self-important somebody, who was irate because a minor official had not known who he was, 'Oh, and who were you?' Busby had the knack of never forgetting a face or a name even on a chance meeting. Paddy Crerand, United's omniscient Scottish international wing-half, related the time shortly after he joined the club when Busby gave permission for his best man Jim Daly, down on a visit from Scotland and a keen United follower, to have lunch with the team on a Saturday before a match against Spurs. He met Busby only briefly, but months later, when United had just beaten Leicester in the Cup Final at Wembley. Busby came out of the dressing room for an interview with the press, and, seeing someone standing beyond the crowd, first went over, shook his hand and asked: 'Well, how are you, Jim?' Never had Jim Daly felt more flattered.

If the most successful manager in the history of the game had faults, those which were discernible were few. Apart from being a poor teller of weak jokes, finding foreign names unpronounceable, and having a voice that wobbled off key during evenings round the piano, he was perhaps over-sensitive to public criticism, blinded no doubt by loyalty to his own cause. As a consequence he was unnecessarily vague sometimes with press and radio over day-to-day matters, which was why local journalists in Manchester often found, without any loss of respect for Old Trafford, that their job was easier over at Maine Road, home of Manchester City. It would, of course, be easy to argue that for the previous 25 years the City had been more in need of friends and publicity than their neighbours, but there existed none the less at Old Trafford a slight air of resentment towards criticism which journalists from London did not encounter. There was a suspicion that journalists in Manchester, to get a pay rise, had to satisfy not only their editors but also Busby.

The most obvious criticism of him was of his failure, to outward appearances, to curb the more unruly elements within the team, which from time to time seriously damaged the club's good name. There were moments, many people felt, when Busby should have publicly made some declaration on his attitude to this kind of behaviour. Yet the public would be wrong to interpret this seeming apathy as lack of discipline within the club. It was one of the myths that Busby was a soft man, an idea that gained momentum through his being seen from time to time celebrating with his players late into the night in a Manchester restaurant or club. Ask any player, and you would be told Busby was as hard as the next man, when it was necessary. The difference was that at Old Trafford the discipline never became public. Famous players were fined heavily, and none left in any doubt when The Boss was displeased. But it was kept private, a tacit understanding between manager and player, so as not to bring the club into further disrepute.

It was partly a question of pride. One of his former players, Noel Cantwell, said: 'You can sense that he is about to say something harsh, then he swallows, holds it back. He does not like to be seen to be angry. But it would come out a day, or two days, later.' Nobby Stiles, a controversial character on the field with a reputation that to an extent exceeded his actual deeds, said that Busby 'does not hand out the toffees' when he called you to his office. If Busby set the standard in civilised treatment of players he never let it override his first principle: that nothing must come before the welfare of the club. When, in 1957, an Italian club tried to buy Tommy Taylor, United's England centre-forward, Busby's answer was emphatic: 'Everything must take second place to the well-being of the club, and if that seems hard on the individual it is unfortunate, but necessary.'

The ability to judge players was Busby's greatest talent of all: always prepared to take calculated risks, and to shoulder the responsibility if the risk failed, always lifting his players up when they were down. Taylor, one of only three players for whom he paid large fees in his first 10 years as manager, perished with seven others of that most famous of all teams in 1958. Yet such was Busby's eye for a player that 12 years after the crash, having himself survived grievous injury, he once more had a pool of 23 first-team players in which only five cost fees. In those 12 years he had spent £700,000 on repairs to the team, some temporary, some permanent, but had re-taken £350,000 in players sold.

It has been said that Busby inherited a team, built a team and bought a team, but in fact there were, in effect, four teams. They were, with transfer fees in brackets:

1948 *(F.A. Cup Winners)*

Crompton

Carey (£250) Aston

Anderson Chilton Cockburn

Delaney (£4,000) Morris Rowley (£3,500) Pearson Mitten

1958 *(Twice League Champions and European Cup semi-finalists, F.A. Cup finalists)*

Wood (£5,000) or Gregg (£24,000)

Foulkes Byrne

Colman Jones or Blanchflower Edwards

Morgan or Viollet Taylor (£30,000) Whelan or Pegg or

Berry (£25,000) Charlton Scanlon

1963 *(F.A. Cup Winners)*

Gaskell

Dunne (£5,000) Cantwell (£30,000)

Crerand (£43,000) Foulkes Setters (£30,000)

Giles Quixall (£45,000) Herd (£40,000) Law (£115,000) Charlton

1968 *(Twice League Champions and European Cup Winners)*

Stepney (£52,000)

Dunne (£5,000) Burns or Brennan

Crerand (£52,000) Foulkes or Sadler Stiles

Best Law (£115,000) or Sadler Charlton Kidd Aston

Four teams: 30 players found for nothing but the effort and patience of travelling thousands of miles to watch hundreds of matches, and 14 others costing £455,750. The work, essentially, of one man. Some years ago Busby said: 'It is the object of life to build. When I knew the worst at Munich I understood at last that to pray for death as I had done was wrong and cowardly. I knew somehow I must succeed again for the sake of those who died. Otherwise my life would have no meaning.' It was my purpose, in 1970, to show something of that life, its meaning, and just how well it succeeded.

—2—
FALTERING FIRST STEPS

Most of us know someone of the kind who goes through life regularly repeating all his mistakes, a danger to himself, failing to learn from experience. One of the obvious and recurring factors in the life of Matt Busby was his ability to turn almost every experience to profit, storing what was beneficial either to himself or to others, rejecting what was shabby or degrading. He did so, moreover, with the minimum of ostentation, so that those who noticed his personality growing did so by observation rather than any unavoidable confrontation. He had not been one to shout, like Archimedes, 'Eureka'; his words, it has been shrewdly observed, followed well in the wake of his thoughts. While he was always slow to condemn, he showed a national thriftiness with praise, which made the award of either a thing to be heeded or cherished.

It is perhaps because he hardly knew his father, killed when he was six, that he was always such a father to those around him, ever since, by some strangely inevitable process, he became an accepted leader. Almost all those who were associated with him benefited from the relationship; he exuded both authority and security; there was a considered, deliberate logic about all he did. Like any boy who grows up from an early age as the eldest male in the family, he was old before his time. Maturity was more of a coat which one day he put on, rather than something which grew on him like bark; and he found it comfortable.

The things he learned as he grew up in football in the late twenties and early thirties were not so much the subtleties of the game as the lessons of life. He noticed the total absence of team-spirit at many clubs, a weakness that came from the top, from the directors and management, while even among the players there was a lack of comradeship, a snobbery which caused those in the first team to ignore the rest. It therefore made that much more of an impression on him when he found, with Liverpool, a generous attitude, in which the playing staff were well treated, always received their benefits when due—which was by no means standard practice—and were even, as in the case of a loyal player Jimmy McDougall, retained on full pay when it was clear that their use to the club the following season was likely to be limited. In the university of humanity Matthew Busby quietly gained an honours degree.

He was born, in 1909, in the tiny mining village of Orbiston, near Bellshill in Lanarkshire, Scotland, in one of 32 two-room cottages, where the bath when his father came in from the pit had to be a bucket on the kitchen floor. In 1916 his father was killed by a sniper's bullet at Arras, so that to bring up the family his mother was obliged to take a job at the pit-head and later, when that closed down, at a steelworks.

At school the young Matthew was proving above average, and was moved at 12 to nearby Motherwell Higher Grade, and such was his promise that the headmaster, a Mr. Bennett, suggested that he should stay until he was 18. However, Mrs. Busby was keen to emigrate to America, where some relations had already gone in the hope of improving their uncertain fortune, and Matthew was sent off to the emigration office. There he was advised that there was a six-month waiting list, so, at 16, he went just where his mother had been hoping to avoid—down the mine. If life below ground was an arduous and unrewarding slog there were compensations up above. From playing with local football team, Orbiston 'Cannibals'—so called, it appears, because of their treatment of any visiting team that had the audacity to win—young Busby graduated to a youth side called Alpine Villa, which won the Scottish Under-18 Cup. When Frank Rogers, a school friend of Busby's, went for a trial with Denny Hibernian, and from there to Manchester City, Busby, after half a dozen games with Denny, followed the same trail. The

Denny secretary was a friend of Jimmy McMullan, the City and Scotland inside-forward; he made the recommendation, and in February 1928 Busby was offered a trial by the City manager, Peter Hodge, with the reserves in the Central League side against Burnley.

Following this, he signed professional forms for a wage of £5 in the season and £4 in summer. When he told his mother, 'there was all hell to pay'. But even in the reserves young Busby found himself out of his depth, struggling manfully but without any great effect as an inside-forward or winger. The first team won the Second Division championship and promotion, but Busby was not heartened, as he went off home for the close season, by the fact that the club had recently signed five new forwards—a misgiving which was confirmed the following season when he made his first brief appearance in the League side against Middlesbrough, only to return immediately to the reserves. Unhappy and homesick, he had on one occasion packed his bags, being restrained by a colleague, Phil McCloy. He wrote to his financée Jean: 'I feel I am out of my sphere in football.' Jean had not believed at first that one really could be *paid* for playing football.

Pneumonia followed, and only the next close season restored his confidence. 'At home,' he recalled, 'I was on top of the world, but in Manchester my confidence deserted me the moment I returned to duty in July. I actually dreaded the approach of each football season.' The following season he scored twice in a Cup replay against Spurs, which City won 4—2, then was retained for the next League game against Bolton, but after a miserable performance was sent back to the reserves. The 1930–1 season was worse than ever, and in the autumn he was not even in the reserves, turning out in the Northern Mid-week League side, which contained mostly amateurs. It was at this time that Manchester United, who in those days were very much the poor relations of City, were hard up for an inside-forward, and the directors told Louis Rocca, the chief scout, to find one, though as cheaply as possible. Rocca contacted Peter Hodge and was told he could have Busby for £150, but had to reply that he could not afford even that, so the deal was off.

With his value and his morale so low, Busby would probably have given up the game, when suddenly there came the turning point. At one of the third-team matches another player failed to arrive, and 20 minutes before the kick-off Busby was told: 'Play at right-half.' By one of those remarkable twists of fate this one incident, precipitated no doubt by some minor hitch in another person's schedule, gave the vital push in the right direction to the man who was to become one of the game's Olympians.

Busby remembered of that afternoon, on some anonymous, deserted pitch somewhere in Lancashire: 'For the first time since coming to England I actually enjoyed a game of football.' Now things moved swiftly. The following Saturday, his improved performance having caught the eye, he was back in the reserves against Sheffield Wednesday. Then, by another stroke of luck following hard on the first, the first-team right-half Barrass was injured and Busby found himself in the League side to play at Huddersfield. Finding his feet at last in his new position, he never looked back from that moment, Barrass being unable to regain his place when he was fit again. It is a story that occurs many times a season in the football world, but never can it have had such significance as on this occasion in the season of 1930–1.

From this experience Busby has never been quick to discard a player of his own, but more important it set a precedent which he many times followed—the switching of a player, usually further back in the team, to exploit a football brain that was unable to express itself in the forward line. Not only was it to prove the making of his own career, but it brought him some of his most notable successes with players he managed—Carey, Aston, Byrne, Blanchflower, Colman, Brennan, Sadler, Burns, and in some ways Charlton.

There was, indirectly, another lesson. On the way to a match one day, one of the Manchester City directors, Bob Smith, said to him confidentially: 'I hope you do well at wing-half—you were a washout as a forward.' Busby appreciated this blunt, direct, but honest comment, and was never himself afraid to be honest with his own players.

Yet though he had at last found himself as a wing-half, it was moving forward with the ball rather than in defence that he shone. One of his colleagues in the City first team was Sid Cann, the right-back. They were two of the first players to gain F.A. Coaching Certificates. After the war Cann became manager of Southampton, nearly taking them to the First Division, and subsequently had notable success with the amateur clubs Wycombe Wanderers and Sutton United—remembered for their meeting with Leeds United, then the current League Champions, in the fourth round of the 1969–70 F.A. Cup, which they lost 6—0.

Of their time together with Manchester City, Cann recalled: 'Matt lived not far from me. He was very reserved, a regular church-goer. He wasn't too sound a defensive player, and his recovery when beaten was a bit slow, as I knew from playing behind him. But he was a fine player to watch in possession, and he would have revelled in a modern mid-field role with freedom to move about and plenty of cover behind him.'

In 1933 Manchester City reached the final of the F.A. Cup, in which they met Everton, and as Cann said, 'we were red-hot favourites'. But misfortune hit City the week before when Freddie Tilson, their centre-forward, was injured in a League match. In the days before the final, when City moved to their London headquarters, Tilson trained in Bushey Park, and on the Friday had a test, after which all the players were confident that he would be fit. Tilson was an important cog in the City machine, and it was a depressing blow to the rest of the side when on the morning of the match the club doctor ruled that Tilson must not play. 'It knocked the stuffing our of most of us,' said Cann.

The player who stepped in for Tilson was Herd, whose son was also to play in a Wembley final—for Manchester United against Leicester City 30 years later. Herd switched from inside forward, his own place being taken by Marshall. City's morale was not improved by arriving at Wembley far too early, almost two hours before the kick-off, and by the time the match began their nerves were so on edge that all confidence was gone. Busby's opposite number in the Everton team was Cliff Britton, later manager of Burnley, Everton and Hull. 'Everton were very much the under-dogs,' said Britton, 'almost as much as Portsmouth against Wolves in 1939 when Portsmouth won 4—1. Everybody in our side clicked right up to half-time. Our big fear was Eric Brook, one of the most dangerous wingers of that time. Matt was not all that conspicuous, as I think he was still making the transition from inside-forward to wing-half.'

Manchester's misfortune pursued them all the way, the first two goals by Everton both being assisted by misjudgment by the City goalkeeper Langford. Twice he failed to measure shots by Britton from outside the penalty area, allowing Everton's outside-left Stein and then their renowned centre-forward Dixie Dean to follow up and score from close in. Dunn, the inside-right, scored again to make it 3—0, the biggest winning margin since the final moved to Wembley in 1923. Teams:

EVERTON

Sagar

Cook   Cresswell

Britton   White   Thomson

Geldard   Dunn   Dean   Johnson   Stein

Brook   McMullan   Herd   Marshall   Toseland

Bray   Cowan   Busby

Dale   Cann

Langford

MANCHESTER CITY

This period was the golden era of Arsenal under Herbert Chapman, and in the five seasons from 1931 to 1935 they won the League Championship four times, the sequence being broken only by Everton in 1932. Manchester City were enjoying mixed fortunes, their positions over the same period being 8th, 14th, 16th, 5th, 4th. It was in the 1933–4 season, when they jumped to fifth, that Busby really began to make an impression on other players, always the true test. It was in this season that Joe Mercer, who over 30 years later was to guide Manchester City back to prosperity, first played against this suddenly blossoming wing-half. Mercer, like

Busby, was an ardent admirer of genuine style, and his face used to light up when he recalled the performances of his contemporary. He would get to his feet in his office and, moving about as he searched his memory, would try to convey an impression of effortlessness.

'What made Matt noticeable was the silkiness in possession, the way he drifted inside from the wing and then switched the ball back over the head of the full-back for his winger. He was a players' player, like Ball or Bell of 30 years later. He had this calm influence on events around him. He always had this, the ability to influence. I remember one match, City against Liverpool, when he was the talk of the dressing room afterwards—pin-pointing his passes uncannily, like Crerand. It wasn't only his accuracy, but the pace was always right. I think Matt and Archie Macaulay were two of the most delicate strikers of the ball there have been.'

It was in 1934, too, that Busby had his first encounter with a man who was to figure prominently with him in the creation of the most successful club of all time—Jimmy Murphy. They were opposite right-halves for Scotland and Wales in the home international championship match at Ninian Park, Cardiff, which was drawn 1—1. Again it was the style of his opponent that remained in Murphy's mind. 'He would have walked through the game today as a linkman. He was a master of the reverse pass, having this marvellous control with his inside foot. I suppose the modern player he was most like in style is Baxter—the same subtlety and ability to do things at his own pace.'

For the second year running City reached the Cup Final, this time against Portsmouth, who had lost to Bolton in 1929. Once again City were dogged by difficulties before the game. Both their regular goalkeepers, Langford and Barber, were injured, and they were obliged to include a virtually untried third-team youngster, Frank Swift. Brought into the League side before the final, he had a poor game against Derby, and was never really tested in the Cup semi-final against Aston Villa, City winning 6—1. It was still with some misgiving that he was included in the team for the final.

At the start of the final it was raining. As he stood there in his goal, before a 100,000 crowd, the 19-year-old Swift must have felt very lonely. It was then that Busby did something which was to prove characteristic. In the first few minutes he suddenly found himself alone and in possession in the penalty area. It should be remembered that in this era it was almost an act of moral cowardice to pass back, but Busby, with unhurried deliberation, rolled the ball back to his young goalkeeper so that he might get his first touch when not under pressure.

Unfortunately his altruism was not sufficient to prevent Swift allowing Rutherford to put Portsmouth ahead with a 'soft' goal after 26 minutes, the ball spinning out of his hands, and try as City would the score remained the same until a quarter of an hour from the end. It was now that fortune frowned on Portsmouth. Allen, their centre-half, was injured in a clash with Cowan, the City centre-half, and was carried off to receive treatment behind the Portsmouth goal. At half-time Tilson, having missed the final the previous year, had reassured his crestfallen 'keeper by saying, 'Don't worry, I'll put two in during the second half.' Now, with Allen still off the field watching helplessly, Tilson scored the equaliser, following a superb move between Busby, Bray and Brook. Tilson calmly picked his spot beyond Gilfillan's reach.

This goal completely swung the game. Portsmouth, even with Allen back on the pitch, were now outplayed. As a thunderstorm broke overhead, City swept on to victory, though it was not until three minutes from time that Tilson kept his promise to Swift and scored the winner. The match even then was not yet over, for Swift had to respond with a memorable save from Portsmouth's inside-right Smith in the last minute. Indeed, Swift was so overcome with nerves that when the referee—who was S. F. Rous, later secretary of the Football Association and then president of F.I.F.A.—finally blew his whistle he fainted and had to be revived before receiving his winner's medal from King George V. The King later wrote to Swift, saying he hoped he had recovered from the ordeal. He had indeed, for he went on to play memorable games for England. As a journalist, he was one of those who died in the Munich crash. The teams in that final were:

MANCHESTER CITY
Swift
Barnett   Dale
Busby   Cowan   Bray
Toseland   Marshall   Tilson   Herd   Brook

Rutherford   Easson   Weddle   J. Smith   Worrall
Thackeray   Allen   Nichol
W. Smith   Mackie
Gilfillan
PORTSMOUTH

In its report of the final the *Daily Telegraph* said: 'Busby, the finest right-half ever seen at Wembley, and Brook inspired the whole side.' After the years of bitter struggle and disillusion Busby was at last recognised as a force in the game, someone to be respected. But his troubles were not over. Although in the next season Manchester City finished fourth in the League, his highest position with them, he was not really happy at the club and, after being out of the game for a while with a leg injury, he thought it might be better for both him and the club if he moved on. He asked for a transfer, which was agreed, and in March 1936 he went for £8,000 to Liverpool, whose hope was that he would help them avoid relegation. The club was in serious difficulty on and off the field. At the same time as Busby arrived, George Kay from West Ham was taken on as manager, and the influence of these two enabled Liverpool to turn the corner.

They finished 19th in the League, with Aston Villa and Blackburn being relegated. The following season it might have seemed that Busby had made the wrong move, for while Liverpool could only improve their League position by one place, Manchester City won the Championship; but the season after that City were relegated. Busby now consolidated his reputation. Cliff Britton, who was still playing half a mile away with Everton, considered 'his influence was most apparent when he moved to Liverpool. They changed from being a hard, direct and rather unsophisticated side to one with a more classical style, and went from strength to strength.' In the last two seasons before the war they finished 11th.

Another opponent at this time, who was to become a formidable obstacle to Busby's managerial success in later years, was Bill Shankly, then a wing-half with Preston. 'If as a boy at that time you wanted to model yourself on anyone,' Shankly recalled, 'there was nobody better to go and watch than Matt.' Then he added roguishly, with that coffee-grinder laugh: 'Mind you, I'm not sure that I'd have had him in my team: he was a bit too gentle.' Yet there was a mutual respect. On one occasion Preston beat Liverpool at Deepdale. Afterwards Busby went up to Shankly and a group of the Preston players as he was leaving the ground. 'That's the way to play, fellows,' he said: 'strength plus ability.' He was not without realisation that physical resilience had its place in the game.

On another occasion, when Liverpool had lost at home to West Bromwich in 1938, he was chatting afterwards to Jimmy Murphy, who was the West Bromwich right-half, and introduced him to Tommy Cooper, the Liverpool and England full-back. 'You always need two pairs of shin-pads when you play against this fellow,' he told Cooper. Perhaps recognising the lack of physical aggression in his own play, he was to select Murphy to be his lieutenant after the war.

At the same time he never wavered from the belief that the fundamental quality for any great team had to be pure skill. This opinion had been reinforced on tour with Liverpool in Czechoslovakia in the summer of 1936. They were beaten 4—1; not luckily but by basic technique. Already the writing was on the wall. The continentals, having been taught the game in the first place by the British, were now overtaking them, largely because of the misplaced emphasis in the domestic British competitions on speed and strength. Only a handful of people in Britain—Arthur Rowe of Spurs, Stanley Rous, Busby, and a few others—realised then the threat which was not finally obvious to all until the Hungarians twice smashed England in 1953 and 1954.

For Busby the player, his career, wartime football apart, was almost at a close. As for so many of the great players of that time, the end of the war found them past their best. For those such as I who did not begin to follow the game until a new generation of stars was emerging afterwards one can best get an idea of the qualities with which Matt Busby delighted pre-war spectators from this appreciation published in the *Manchester Guardian* in 1934. With startling accuracy, I think it captures every significant characteristic of this remarkable man:

'At best, he has no superior as an attacking half-back. It is his bewildering footcraft which most delights the crowds. His crouching style may not be pretty but the control is perfect, the affect akin to conjuring. His dribble is a thing of swerves, feints and deceptions. Few opponents are not hoodwinked by his phantom pass. Even the real one is nearly always masked. It skids off to the right when one could swear it was destined for the centre. Busby scorns the obvious. His passes not only look good, they sound good. There is that same healthy thwack of leather that means a scurry in the outfield in a cricket match.

Busby is not so sound in defence. A lack of speed he cloaks in shrewd positional play, so that he intercepts more often than he tackles, but it is a flaw in his armour. Some would find another in the spirit of adventure which will not be repressed even in front of his own goal. Sometimes he does dare-devil things that make the directors feel old before their time. But who would have him different? He laughs equally at his blunders and his triumphs, which of course is the privilege as well as the proof of a great player. He would be a certain choice for that select eleven of Footballers Who Obviously Love Football—and that is the highest praise of all.'

—3—
ASSUMING COMMAND

Just after Manchester United had won the F.A. Cup in 1948, giving Matt Busby his first real taste of success as a manager, the club departed for a summer tour in Northern Ireland. They were due to play a match in Bangor, and their accommodation had been arranged in a small hotel belonging to an official of the Irish Football Association. He was not a very important official, and it was not a very big hotel, hardly grand enough, in fact, for the F.A. Cup winners. But the proprietor had carefully and with great pride prepared for the visit for some weeks, for it was to be one of the biggest events the little Irish town had seen for a long while. As the day of the team's arrival approached, extra food was ordered—for food even in hotels was still short in those days—and everything was ready.

When the team landed off the boat at Belfast it so happened that while they went straight to the hotel in Bangor by coach, Busby had gone separately by car with some members of the Irish F.A., probably for a drink before lunch. When the players arrived at the hotel, they went to check in to their rooms and it was quickly obvious that things were not quite what they were used to. Two of the players were sharing an attic where there was no window, only a skylight, and there were various other things wrong. Soon the players began to gather downstairs again, and started to moan in the way that players do when everything isn't just so. Johnny Carey, the captain, tried to reason with them that they should 'give it a go'; that as the proprietor had gone to so much trouble, and was not really doing it for the money but the goodwill, they should put on a smile.

Accompanying the team was Bill Petherbridge, a new Manchester United director. It should be remembered that at this time directors were still very much 'employers', and that the players and even the manager were the hired servants of the club. At any rate, Mr. Petherbridge, no doubt with the best intentions for the comfort of his team, called out to the assembled group: 'Stop! We're not staying here. We'll find somewhere more suitable. Bring all the bags down.'

It was at this point that Busby suddenly arrived on the scene. He took one look around at what was happening, and then turned on Mr. Petherbridge. 'He was absolutely furious,' one of the United players recalls.

'Look here,' exploded Busby, 'we cannot possibly walk out like this. It is disgraceful. I won't have it.' The United players stood looking on, dumbfounded. It was unprecedented for a manager to address one of his directors in this way, and no one could be quite sure what was going to happen next. Unfortunately, the proprietor of the hotel was by this time already so upset that rather than face further embarrassment the team did leave for another hotel.

This incident, one of the few occasions on which Busby had been known to show emotion in public, clearly indicates that he was even then, after only three years in the managerial chair at Old Trafford, in no doubt as to who was The Boss. He himself had said that 'I made it quite plain to them that I was to be in sole charge of all affairs connected with the team. If it did not work out, they could fire me,' Strange to think that only a few years back, during the bleak uncertainty of wartime, he had many a time been sitting around waiting to find out if he could get 30 shillings (£1.50) as a 'guest' player for Doncaster Rovers.

Yet it was in the war that his qualities of leadership off the field first emerged. One of those who served with him remarked that 'he was a rock-like, dependable fellow, hard when he had to be'. A large part of the time he spent as Army P.T. instructor on troopships in convoy to and from the Mediterranean, attempting to maintain morale, both physical and mental, and to dispel boredom. His job was made none the easier on account of the fact that he was one of world's worst sailors. 'He'd have been sick crossing the Mersey' was Mercer's opinion.

Following the invasion of Italy by Allied troops, Matt was given command of the Army football team, their job being to tour, often not far behind the line, providing entertainment for the troops. His squad included many well-known names: Bacuzzi, Britton, Elliott, Lawton, Mercer, Mullen, Rowe (his second-in-command), Rowley, George Smith, Sproston, Swift, and Watson. Joe Mercer was in charge of rations, partly on account of his ability, it seems, to scrounge food from the most improbable sources, partly because he possessed the only tin-opener. When this was lost, Cliff Britton came to the rescue. He was in charge of transport—and proceeded to drive their truck over the tins, which soon opened them.

Busby was both a firm and tolerant leader. There were the inevitable escapades and at one time he had to tell the party: 'This tour is for the benefit of other people as well as you—keep in line.' On the other hand, Arthur Rowe recalls the time when he followed up a couple of rare gin-and-tonics at an officers' mess with supper for the day, which was corned-beef sandwiches, and was dreadfully sick all night. Matt, in the bunk underneath, never made a murmur of complaint.

On the field he was the model of diplomacy. When the team went on to Athens they played the first football match after the liberation, and it didn't take the Greeks long to get excited. The match was ref-ereed by a naval officer in white shorts, cravat . . . and a hat. At one stage he gave an indirect free-kick *inside* the penalty area. The Greek team had never encountered this before and there was soon pande-monium. Matt, weighing up the situation, quickly took the kick, put it wide of the goal for a goal-kick, collected the ball, placed it, and waved the Greek 'keeper to play on.

It was during this Army tour that Busby again met Jimmy Mur-phy. When the team was at Bari, in south-east Italy, prior to crossing to Athens, Busby saw Murphy instructing a group of soldiers, went over to chat, and told him that if he was interested there would be a job for him as assistant at Old Trafford as soon as Murphy was back in civvies.

Busby had been appointed manager of Manchester United just before the touring side left London. Liverpool had been anxious to

retain him as a player-coach, an appointment which he accepted ver-
bally, but meanwhile he was offered the post at Old Trafford by J.
W. Gibson, the chairman. With Liverpool's reluctant consent he
decided to take this seemingly thankless job. Liverpool, at first asking him to play in a farewell exhibition match, abruptly cancelled
the invitation.

On the face of things the situation at Old Trafford was desperate.
There was an overdraft of £15,000, no small matter in those days
when the record transfer fee stood at £14,000. The ground lay
almost derelict, destroyed by bombs in 1941. The offices had been
transferred to the premises of the chairman's firm. There was
nowhere to train but the car park. For the time being matches were
played at the City ground at Maine Road. Last and possibly most
discouraging of all, Manchester United's immediate pre-war record
was anything but impressive—Second Division champions in 1936,
relegated the following year, promoted again with Aston Villa in
1938, and 14th in the First Division in 1939.

Busby, however, knew where he was going. 'I wanted,' he said
later, 'a different kind of football club from what was normal at the
time. There wasn't a human approach. I wanted to manage a team
the way I thought the players wanted it. In those days the atmosphere in clubs was bad. The first team would hardly recognise the
lads underneath. The manager sat at his desk and you saw him once
a week.' His effect on the team was instant. Here was a man prepared to hunt with his hounds, getting down to work with them in
a track-suit. Team talks were not a moral five-minute lecture a quarter of an hour before Saturday's kick-off, but took place several times
during the week. The players could even voice an opinion. 'If you
made a suggestion,' John Aston recalled, 'he might appear not to
notice, but the next day he'd say, "I've been thinking about what
you said," and then give his reason for doing it, or not.'

In his first season Busby showed his flair for taking a gamble. For
£4,000 he bought Jimmy Delaney from Celtic, even though Delaney
had a suspect injured shoulder and was getting old for a winger.
Delaney, one of the most entertaining of players, with a perplexing
dribble and little hair, gave United four years of valuable service. He

drew appreciation wherever he played. I remember one occasion against Chelsea at Stamford Bridge. Setting off on one of his runs, Delaney beat one man. 'Nice,' said a Chelsea supporter. Delaney beat a second man. 'Nice,' said the supporter again. Casually, almost lazily, Delaney went past a third. Without emotion, the spectator added with the air of an headmaster: 'Now craws it, skin'ead'— which Delaney unerringly did and Chelsea were one down.

At the end of Busby's first season, 1945–6, United finished fourth in the temporary Northern League with the following team:

Crompton

Hamlett   Chilton

Aston   Whalley   Cockburn

Delaney   Pearson   Rowley   Buckle   Wrigglesworth

The following season, Carey, Morris, Mitten and others returned from the Services. Carey, the club captain, and Busby formed one of the great partnerships, comparable to Nicholson and Blanchflower for Spurs a decade later. Carey had come to United by accident. In 1936 Louis Rocca, the chief scout, went over to Ireland to look at a player recommended by the club's representative there. But the player in question was injured, so instead Rocca went to see another youngster playing with St. James Gate, the team of the Guinness firm. Rocca signed him on the spot. In fact Carey had played for Eire before he joined United, and it was in a wartime international friendly match against the British Army that he first met Busby. Carey was centre-forward for Ireland, Busby centre-half for the Army. Busby chatted to him throughout the match, saying at one stage: 'It's odd, but I've always regarded you as a half-back.'

As soon as Carey returned to full-time football, Busby made the first of many positional switches that were to prove so perceptive. he converted the two Johns, Carey and Aston, from inside-forwards to full-backs. It was an entirely new concept of the game, as Carey recalled. 'Other people had always said that with two wing-halves, two inside-forwards, a goal-keeper and a centre-half, you had a team. We now tried to create the game from the back. Our wing-halves, Anderson and Cockburn, were more the ranging destroyers.'

Again, Busby was ahead of the Hungarians and Dutch.

Yet always Busby was looking for variation. On one occasion he said to Carey: 'Look, you're one of the best kickers of the ball in the game. I want you to use the long ball more often. Don't always play it short.' In the next match, against Huddersfield, Carey hit the first ball that came to him straight down the middle, Rowley scored, and United won 5—0. United finished the season runners-up to Liverpool, one point behind, and ahead of Wolves on goal average—and with a £60,000 profit.

It was during this season that Busby first demonstrated that it was he and not the directors who was in charge. At Easter, after a 3—0 'home' win at Maine Road—where United played all their home games until August 1949—the directors wanted to change the team in spite of the victory. Hints were dropped, and most of the players knew what was afoot, waiting to see where the blow would fall for the match the following day. But Busby insisted that the team should be unchanged, and told his players: '*I* pick this side.'

In 1947–8 United were again runners-up in the League, this time to Arsenal, and again it was goal average that nosed them in front of Burnley in third place. What will always be remembered this season, however, is their performance in the Cup, crowned with victory in the final over Blackpool. It is often said that this was the team which Busby 'inherited', yet including positional switches there were seven changes from the time when he took over, and it was unquestionably 'his' side as much as any of those to come.

A match which those who saw it claim was one of the most exciting ever played was United's first tie on the way to Wembley, at Villa Park in the third round. The correspondent of *The Times*, Geoffrey Green, had previously backed United to win the Cup at 28—1, but had unfortunately tipped Villa as the other finalists. A 60,000 crowd was gathered for the start in teeming rain. Within 10 seconds of the kick-off United were one down without having touched the ball, Villa sweeping through for Edwards to score. Carey's only reaction was to put his hands on his hips, look at the ball in the back of the net, *and smile*: by half-time United were leading 5—1. Then in the second half Villa fought back through the mud to make it 5—4 with

10 minutes to go. The pace and the skill was remarkable, remembering that in those days there was no waterproof ball. With two minutes to go Preston made it 6—4 from a corner as the roar of the Villa crowd surged across the ground, desperate for the equaliser.

United went on to reach the final with vintage football, scoring 18 goals to six on the way: Aston Villa 6—4, Liverpool 3—0, Charlton 2—0, Preston 4—1, and Derby 3—1 at Hillsborough, all First Division teams.

Before the semi-final it has been rumoured that Derby were on a bonus of £100 a man to win, the maximum wage at this time being £14 a week, and any bonus of this kind illegal. The United players persuaded Carey to approach Busby to see if there was the chance of a similar 'incentive' for them. His answer was an adamant no, yet he still managed, as one of the team says now, 'to get us to the final in the right frame of mind'.

In his pre-match tactical talk 'he first of all gave us an impression of confidence in our ability. It was our qualities he stressed rather than the opposition's'—this in spite of the fact that the opposition contained two of the England attack, Matthews and Mortensen. Busby's strategy with Matthews was, as far as possible, to 'freeze' him out of the game. United would play predominantly to their right, away from Blackpool's right flank, especially at free-kicks and clearances from Crompton in goal. In addition Mitten, United's outside left, was to drop back where possible to assist Aston in checking Matthews. All this sounds simple enough in modern tactical thinking, but in 1948 it was highly advanced.

At the start things did not go well for United. When Chilton brought down Mortensen with a sliding tackle from behind, a penalty was awarded and Shimwell, the Blackpool right-back, scored from the spot. Yet stills from film of the incident showed conclusively afterwards that Chilton's tackle had been made in the 10-yard arc on the front of the area . . . *outside*. Before half-time Rowley made it 1–1, but once again Mortensen put Blackpool ahead, and this was still the position with 20 minutes to go. Then United produced a sustained spell of pressure which few teams could have withstood. A header by Rowley from Morris's quick free-kick made the score level, Pearson put United ahead for the first time and a long-range drive by Anderson put them beyond reach. For the first time at Wembley a team had been twice behind and won. All the time United had been down, Carey had directed: 'Don't panic, keep playing football.' It is to this day talked of as one of the best Wembley finals. The teams were:

MANCHESTER UNITED

Crompton

Carey   Aston

Anderson   Chilton   Cockburn

Delaney   Morris   Rowley   Pearson   Mitten

Rickett   Dick   Mortensen   Munro   Matthews

Kelly   Hayward   Johnston

Crossland   Shimwell

Robinson

BLACKPOOL

Elated as he must have been at his triumph coming so soon, Busby let others do most of the celebrating. He knew there was still a long way to go. As Johnny Carey said: 'He never used a superlative about something that didn't deserve it. Very occasionally after a match, aside, he would come and say "Well done, skipper", which meant more than a thousand pounds. You had to win his heart. I don't suppose he said it more than four or five times in seven years. I always tried to play in such a way as to *make* him say it.' One of those few occasions was when United beat Rangers in the 1953 Coronation Cup at Hampden.

Pleased as the players were after Wembley, there was trouble before the start of the next season—on the Thursday before the first match they went on strike, refusing to train. For winning the Cup in 1946, Derby, it was said, had been rewarded with gold watches in addition to the legal bonus of £20. The United players, smarting with a sense of injustice, forced a meeting, against Busby's will, with the directors. It was held in the dressing-room. Harold Hardman, the chairman, patiently explained that any extra payment or gift was against the regulations, and the club would not break them. One of the players suggested, as a means of getting round this, that each player should be given a set of golf clubs—for training. But the directors held their ground, the players went disgruntled into the first match, and were beaten 2—1 at home . . . by Derby. 'We were spectators for most of the game,' recalls John Aston.

If Busby would not break the rules at least he was determined to exploit them to the fullest extent in the players' favour where possible, as another incident during that season demonstrated. Just as today, the time when the word gets round about what sort of money players are getting at other clubs is at international matches. It happened that Aston shared a room with Tom Finney of Preston before an England game, and learned that although they were only in their fourth post-war season, time spent as an amateur on a club's books before the war could be taken into consideration for qualifying for a five-year benefit—which applied in Aston's case.

When he got back to Old Trafford, he went straight to see Busby and asked if this was so. 'No,' answered Busby. Aston explained that Finney has received a benefit in this way. Immediately Busby hurried next door into the office of Walter Crickmer, the secretary. 'Is this true?' he demanded. Crickmer replied that it was. As in Bangor, it was obvious that Busby was highly annoyed. 'How many times have I said that these players are to get every penny they are entitled to?' he said tartly, and promptly arranged back-dated benefits for seven or eight of the team.

He went even further than this. Benefits were shortly given to several of the club's youngsters who were not yet even 21—Whitefoot, Jones, Viollet, and others. This was quite unheard of, and caused so many raised eyebrows at other clubs that the rule was altered at the next annual general meeting.

The defeat in that opening game of the 1948–9 season against Derby was the start of a moderate autumn for United, in which there were several unexpected defeats. A national daily newspaper had to publish an apology for suggesting that Busby had 'agreed that defeat by Derby had done the team good as they were getting big-headed'. In fact the team recovered well to finish runners-up for the third consecutive year, this time to Portsmouth; for the third time running, too, goal average was decisive, placing them ahead of Derby.

In April 1949 Busby was offered the post of manager at Tottenham at a salary reported to be £2,750. He turned it down. He was already involved in the most exciting phase of his whole career. At the end of the 1947 season Jimmy Murphy, who was managing the reserve team, had told him: 'Although we have won the Central League, not one of the players is good enough for the first team.' So then and there Busby and Murphy started to build a dream—a dream which was to become a breathtaking reality.

—4—

BUILDING A DREAM

In 25 years at Old Trafford there had been few players with whom Matt Busby had not had a sympathetic understanding. Even with the difficult characters he had usually managed to establish a workable relationship, provided that he felt the player was valuable to the performance of the team as a whole. But one player whose temperament he was seldom able to fathom was his inside-right in that first Cup Final, Johnny Morris.

One of the qualities which made that team so formidable was the contrast between the characteristics of the players, and nowhere was this more marked than at inside-forward, where Morris had the nimble technique and Stan Pearson the cunning footballer's brain. Morris was popular with the crowd, extrovert and entertaining: Pearson studious, dependable and a shrewd tactician. Morris was also a tough player. Murphy recalls that he had 'never played against a forward who goes in so hard for the ball', and Murphy was no thistle-down.

Try as Busby would, however, he could not strike up harmony with this tormentor of defences. He confided in one of his other players: 'I've tried every angle. I've bullied, I've used flattery, I've tried every way, but I just can't get through.' A typical instance of their differences occurred at training one day. In a League match Blackpool had scored a goal against United direct from a free-kick, and the following Tuesday Busby was practising lining up the wall to try to ensure that this did not happen again. He felt that if they had five men in the wall, instead of four, this would do the trick. They rehearsed the situation from many different positions, and Busby seemed satisfied. It was past the time to stop, and the players were keen to get off to lunch.

Morris, however, was not convinced. 'I still think it's possible to score, even with a five-man wall,' he insisted. Busby, thinly concealing his irritation at Morris's seeming impertinence, said, 'Right then, you'd better show us.' Once more the line formed up—and Morris calmly smashed the ball past it, past the goalkeeper, and into the top of the net, all with the disdain of a Pele or Eusebio. It was hardly surprising that such irritations snow-balled, till they reached the point where there was not room for both Busby and Morris, and the inside-forward was transferred to Derby for £25,000. No manager, right or wrong, can have his authority questioned too often. It is essential that all must pull together.

Busby knew that he could afford to let Morris go, because although on the face of things he had one of the most successful teams in the country, behind the scenes the production wheels were already turning in the most ambitious experiment a football club had ever attempted. 'I was lucky to have such players at my disposal when I first joined the club,' Busby wrote later, 'but I realised you need more than luck to survive. I wanted to achieve a sound club, and I knew I would need a lot of good young players to help me in my plans. I never wanted Manchester United to be second to anybody. Only the best would be good enough. I had to have players who would play for me and United, rather than for themselves.'

It was not long after the war before people began to ask where were the players who were to succeed Mercer, Cullis, Carter, Matthews and the rest. Busby had his own idea. He considered that if one combed the country for the pick of the schoolboys when they were leaving at 15, not only would he save expensive transfer fees later on but he would be able to mould the players as they matured to his own pattern. More than that, he was looking for that burning dedication to a cause, that kind of fanatic loyalty which was previously only found in some of the great amateur teams, stemming from the public schools, such as the Corinthians, and in his own Scottish national team, with its special brand of fiery patriotism.

To help him achieve his ambition Busby had gathered round him a select staff: Jimmy Murphy, that jovial, tough and experienced Welsh international, who managed the reserves and also helped to assess schoolboy players, once they had been recommended; Bert Whalley, former United centre-half, who supervised the coaching of the youngsters; and Joe Armstrong, former G.P.O. engineer whose eye for potential in a schoolboy made him the most valuable scout in the business.

'Matt is a shrewd user of people,' Cliff Lloyd said. In these three assistants, plus a handful of carefully selected scouts, Busby had formed a team which created a conveyor belt carrying the most talented boys in England, Scotland, Ireland and Wales from the classroom to the Manchester United first team. It was a system, a machine, which other clubs came to envy, fear, and resent. Busby himself said: 'I did not set out to build a team: the task ahead was much bigger than that. What I really embarked upon was the building of a system which would produce not one team but four or five, each occupying a rung on the ladder, the summit of which was the first XI.'

Murphy, in some ways, was the more complete man and was closer to the players than Busby, who tended to be respected from a distance; the difference between brother and father. While Busby had the vision, and embodied the idealism of his ambitions, Murphy had the more intimate day-to-day contact with all but the first team, and therefore in one sense knew them better. While Busby directed their destiny, Murphy played a greater part in fashioning the raw material. To those close to him Murphy admitted that, possibly, at the highest level, he would not have made a manager. Lacking Busby's great diplomacy, Murphy might have thundered into certain situations in a way which would have alienated his best friends. Busby, immensely warm yet somehow detached, has always been slightly remote from the players with whom he has had this close mutual respect. 'Although you can get to know him well,' an acquaintance of his outside football said, 'you can get so far and no further.' The economic severity of his youth and his preoccupation with his life's purpose probably inhibited his capacity for the more casual involvement that clutters the path of most of us.

Armstrong, a small, elfish man with curling grey hair and a mischievous smile, had been a part-time scout with Manchester City, and was invited by Busby to join United after the war. He was then already 52, yet showing the energy and enthusiasm of men half his age set about covering thousands of miles in the hunt that was now on. Much of this travelling was by car with Busby, who, he said, 'must be the world's worst navigator'. Returning from West Kirby on one occasion at midnight after attempting to sign a boy, they stopped in Chester for some fish and chips. With Busby driving, they set off again for Manchester, with Murphy fast asleep in the back. Twenty minutes later they were back in Chester.

Among other things, Busby realised that if young boys were to be encouraged to come to Old Trafford their welfare away from the club had to be looked after. A select band of landladies was chosen, those who could be depended upon to make Manchester a home from home for a boy suddenly removed from the reassuring surroundings of his own town. Where possible the boys were encouraged to study for an alternative career; they were sent home to see their parents at weekends whenever the fixture schedule permitted. Most important of all, a boy was never signed unless Busby was confident he would make the grade. The key question in any interview was always, 'Do you *want* to join Manchester United?'

Far from having a vast army of scouts, as many people supposed, United had only eight, and as Busby recalled: 'The going was hard in the early days. I travelled the length and breadth of the British Isles to watch school teams, youth teams, works teams, even Water Board teams.' Over three-quarters of the tip-offs the club received, Armstrong says, were from schoolmasters who had some connection with the club or were merely keen supporters. One of these was a former Swinton man, a Mr. Hemingway, who wrote from Ashington in Northumberland saying he had a boy whom he thought was promising. Busby sent Armstrong to have a look. On a gloomy, frosty February morning Armstrong stood shivering as East Northumberland played Jarrow and Hebburn, but he came away realising he had just seen one of the most exciting prospects of all his many hours of often unrewarding drudgery . . . Bobby Charlton.

When in 1953, Charlton played for England Schoolboys against Scotland at Wembley, scoring two goals, there were 18 clubs in the queue for his signature. It seemed that his most likely and natural destination would be Newcastle, but his uncle, no less than the famous Jackie Milburn—who had led Newcastle to victory in the Cup Final for the past two years—advised young Bobby that the club had internal troubles that made the future unhealthy. Armstrong having followed him around for weeks, almost to the point of sitting outside his bedroom, Charlton finally settled for Manchester United.

When he first moved to Manchester, Charlton was apprenticed at an engineering works, which was thought a proper safeguard even for one so outstanding. This was no fun; he had to be up at 7.30 every morning, bitterly envying some of the others who were merely required to arrive at the ground in time for training. This continued till he was 17. It was a sign of the times, and the still widely held notion that football clubs bought and sold players over their heads, when one day at the works the foremen said to Charlton: 'Do you know that United have signed you as a professional?' having just read the papers. Though now a fully fledged professional, it was a hard life for the boy who was to become one of the most admired players in the world over the next 10 years. He recalls that 'Duncan Edwards gave me one of his shirts—not because, as he said, it was too small for him, but because I think he thought I needed it more than he did.'

There were many stars who were caught in the Old Trafford net, but the brightest three without doubt were Edwards, Charlton and later George Best. Those whose experience has spanned the game both before and after the war say there has never been another like Edwards—a giant in physique, performance and psychological value to his side. As with Charlton, there had been a swarm of clubs chasing him, though it seemed that, coming from Dudley, he would inevitably move to Wolverhampton Wanderers, only a few miles away. Stan Cullis, the Wolves manager, aware that Edwards received inducements, was furious.

Busby's interest was first aroused by Joe Mercer, who had been

appointed the first professional coach to the English Schools XI.
Busby at the time was interested in a boy named Farrell, who was in
the side under Mercer's care, and asked his opinion. Mercer replied:
'I don't think you have a chance with him because he's set on going
to Everton. Besides, there's only one to think about in this side—
Edwards.' So Armstrong, Whalley and Murphy got on the trail, and
eventually were able to entice Edwards away from under the nose of
Wolves. It was the biggest scoop of all, and caused no end of resentment. The decisive factor was, as Busby liked to say, 'Duncan's own
burning desire to play for Manchester United'—perhaps partly true.
Just as Farrell could think only of Everton, so Edwards idolised
United. Even so, he was finally hauled out of bed to sign in the small
hours of the morning after Murphy had heard that another club was
making a desperate last bid to persuade him to change his mind.

Another link in the chain Busby was forging was Eddie Colman,
who was captured at about this time, almost on United's doorstep.
Small, but with wonderful control and a swerve that came from the
hips and could shift opponents as if mesmerised, Colman came to
form a memorable wing-half partnership with Edwards; brilliant in
its contrast like that between Morris and Pearson previously at
inside-forward, and later Mackay and Danny Blanchflower of
Spurs. With the departure of Carey and Aston at full-back, the creative emphasis reverted to wing-half. Busby said of Colman: 'I had
seen hundreds of schoolboy footballers, many capped several times
by their countries, yet none impressed me at first glance quite so
forcibly as Colman.'

All these boys may have been outstanding when they arrived at
Old Trafford, for their age the cream of the country, but there was
still much work to be done on them. Hours of patient coaching by
Whalley and Murphy instilled into them the necessary tactical disciplines, so that when they came to play together their natural and
separate talents would blend instinctively. With none was this more
necessary than Charlton.

Devastating near goal, with perfection of timing in either foot
which gave him a fearsome shot, Charlton had to be taught that
there was a middle of the pitch as well as a goal-mouth, and that this

was where the battle was primarily waged. Being such a fluent striker of the ball, it was Charlton's tendency to hit a stream of long passes to the wings, of value at times but often risky and squandering possession. Countless times Murphy would have to take him on one side and say: 'Play it short, play it short. You *must* first master the short game.' It was not Charlton's instinct—so acute, for example in Dennis Law—to give a pass and go for the return. It was almost 10 years before Charlton finally became a key player in mid-field for both his club and country, following a long and erratic spell first as inside-forward and then winger.

However long the time spent in schooling the boys to the new world of professional soccer, Busby and Murphy never resorted to the line of so many managers — 'This is how *we* used to do it.' Murphy, however, unselfishly helped foster the awe in which Busby was held by the juniors. Charlton, who first met Busby at a schoolboys' international trial, had been at first surprised at his reputation, 'when it seemed that everyone else was doing all the work'. Once he began to play it was different. 'I remember almost trembling in my boots,' he says, 'if we heard that he was coming to watch the youth team. Jimmy would say, "You've got to do well tonight," and everyone would be on edge. He was a legendary figure, part of the world we never stopped dreaming about. His presence seemed to electrify all of us. We would tear into the game like lions. It was the only way, in a sense, that we could communicate with him at that time. We would all have run ourselves into the ground for him.'

Almost beyond his dream, Busby had already created the fanatical loyalty he sought. Somehow, too, he conveyed to his young players a feeling of security—a feeling that if they lost, then it was his problem rather than theirs. They rewarded him by winning the new F.A. Youth Cup for the first five years in a row from 1953 to 1957. But we have run slightly ahead of the story.

In the season 1949–50 the first team finished fourth, and the following season second once more—the fourth time in five years—the title being taken by Spurs, now managed by Busby's Army team second-in-command, Arthur Rowe. He, like Busby, was trying to instil a method based on pure skill, conscious of the rising threat from the continent. The style of his team, which included the future England team manager, Alf Ramsey, at right-back, was based on the same principle which Murphy was to try to pump into young Charlton—'push-and-run', Rowe called it: the simple, short-ball game.

At one point on the way to winning the title Rowe told Busby that he felt they had been lucky to have avoided injury. 'That's because you have been making the ball do the work. Keep it up,' Busby replied. It was during this season that United lost 2—0 at home to Birmingham. The man to do the damage was Birmingham's little outside-right Johnny Berry, who gave their defence a roasting. Busby determined that he would try to secure Berry's services, so that he might do the same for them. After enquiries over many months, he was finally told that he could have Berry for £25,000, and he proved to be a vital factor when, at last, United won the League Championship in his first season, 1951–2.

Berry had come into the professional game by accident. He had been a cinema projectionist in Aldershot at the outbreak of war, and when he joined the Army, played football as a way of avoiding some of the chores. During this time he signed amateur forms for Birmingham City while stationed in the Midlands, and rather drifted into professionalism when the war finished. As a dribbler he was almost in the Matthews or Finney class, and he was also a consistent goalscorer. Nevertheless, he was a problem. So great was his ability with the ball that he tended to play 'on his own', disrupting the rhythm of the rest of the side, slowing the game down.

Right from the start, one of Busby's catch-phrases with United was 'nobody in our team stops the ball except the goal-keeper'. Berry seemed not to have heard this, so one day Busby acted. After lunch at the Daveyhulme Golf Club, where the team always went before a home match on a Saturday, Busby waded into Berry in a quite uncharacteristic way. 'Cross that ball, or you're out of the team,' he told him sternly. On the way to the ground Carey said to Busby: 'You've really upset Johnny. He won't be much use to us today.' Busby replied: 'I don't care. I meant to.' He had judged his man better than Carey thought, for Berry had one of his best games ever and United won by three goals.

Berry, whose career was finished by injuries received in the Munich crash, recalled: 'The great thing as a player was that you could tell, just from the practice games on Tuesday, that The Boss must have been a good player himself. He'd give you your head while things went well, but he'd soon be cross if he suggested something and you ignored it. Oh yes, he'd do his nut at times. But usually in private. You could see he was angry sometimes with the youngsters, but he'd control it. He had great patience.'

At the end of the 1949–50 season United had lost their outside-left Mitten. The team went on a summer tour to the United States, and it was about this time that several outstanding English players, notably Neil Franklin, the Stoke and England centre-half, were being tempted by the promise of sky-high wages to go and play in Bogotà, Columbia. Busby warned all his players of the risks involved; that if they broke their contracts by going they would be suspended by F.I.F.A., the international body, and would certainly lose their place at Old Trafford. But while United were in America, Mitten was approached by a representative of Bogotà, and, telling Busby that he could not turn down such a lucrative offer, decided to give it a try. It failed, and after returning to England, Mitten was transferred to Fulham.

It is worth noting here that it was on this 1950 tour that Busby first became attracted to the idea of testing his team out against foreign opposition in competitive conditions in order to extend the range of their experience. But the point about the departure of Mitten was that it opened the way for the first of Busby's youngsters, Roger Byrne. He had been signed in 1948, and gained a regular place at outside-left in the team that won the Championship in 1952. Another change during this season was in goal. Crompton was out of the side for three months with a wrist injury, Allen taking over. It was the kind of situation in which any player becomes depressed, but Crompton recalled that Busby 'made continuous efforts to ensure that I was kept interested and busy, that I was not idle at the weekends. It would have been so easy to feel out of things with the rest of the team on the crest of a wave, but The Boss made sure I didn't.'

There was a distinct chance this season that Arsenal would win the double of League and Cup, but in the Cup Final they were beaten by Newcastle 1—0, after Barnes, their right-back, was injured early on. In the League Arsenal had a marvellous run, being unbeaten from December 29 to April 21. On April 26 they came to Old Trafford needing to win 7—0 to take the title—and were beaten 6—0. Manchester United were Champions for the first time for 41 years. In his first seven years as manager Busby had lifted both the major trophies, not to mention finishing second in the League four times. The team in that season was (3–3–4):

Allen (or Crompton)

McNulty   Chilton   Aston

Carey   Downie   Cockburn

Berry   Rowley   Pearson   Byrne

The following season marked the retirement of Johnny Carey, and although it was only three years since he had had his last benefit Busby decided that he was entitled to three-fifths of a second. For the first time in his 10 years there, Carey was invited to the board room and there was a small celebration with the directors. If this sounds insignificant in these egalitarian days, it was then a substantial honour, and Carey was most moved. In his 10 seasons he had played in nine positions at one time or another—one of the outstanding players of all time.

Six months after winning the Championship, United were at the foot of the table. Others beside Carey were getting old. Busby pacified the annual shareholders' meeting by telling them: 'There is no need to worry. We have £200,000 worth of talent in the youth and reserve teams.' This was, in those days and at current transfer fees, a startling statement, but Busby and Murphy were confident it was true. Indeed they had already agreed that five of the Central League side were ready to be drafted into the first team when the moment was right. This came in a friendly match against Kilmarnock. After telling the directors what he was about to do, Busby made sweeping changes. In came the pick of his youngsters—Whitefoot, Jackie Blanchflower, Colman, Edwards, Pegg. As Busby said, 'I intend making the move which is going to make or break Manchester United.'

In one blow a great but ageing team had been replaced. The youngsters did not fail their manager; Kilmarnock were beaten 3—0. At great risk, Busby kept the side for the next two matches against Huddersfield and Arsenal, and both were drawn. The gamble had succeeded. In a shorter time than he had hoped Busby had almost realised his dream. Keeping his fingers crossed, telling the players to keep their heads and play their normal game, Busby kept them in for most of the rest of the season, and the side finished a respectable eighth.

Meanwhile those who had been replaced were not dumped on the scrap-heap. Once more setting the standard in professional ethics, Busby allowed them to go for little or no fee to clubs where their skills could still be of value—Chilton and Rowley as player-managers respectively of Grimsby and Plymouth, Cockburn and Pearson to Bury, Delaney back to Scotland.

There were two other important changes during this season: the formation of a new full-back partnership, Foulkes and Byrne, which if it did not equal Carey and Aston in technique made up for it in tenacity. Busby made another of his inspired switches and, following the pattern set with Carey and Aston, moved Byrne from outside-left to left-back. Here he proved himself an immediate success. Although none too sound in the air, his positional and tactical sense and his powers of recovery were extraordinary. Within a year Busby made him club captain, and from the moment he was selected for England against Scotland, on April 3, 1954, he played in 33 consecutive internationals, including the World Cup series in Switzerland, before his death in the Munich crash.

Bill Foulkes, the son of a miner and himself working at the mine when signed by Murphy in 1950 at 17, had made his first League appearance against Liverpool in December 1952, having to mark the famous Billy Liddell. For Foulkes—next to Busby and Murphy themselves, the most solid part of the Old Trafford framework over the next 20 years—it was a bit of a gamble in 1950. At the pit he was earning £15; as a youngster with United he received £7, but he weighed up the prospects and made the right choice. He recalled that Busby said very little to him when throwing him in at the deep end against Liverpool. 'He just asked, "Are you happy about it?" and I must have said yes, so he simply added: "Right, then in you go." He had this knack of handing the responsibility over to you, of treating you like a man. He didn't try to fill your head with theory. In a strange way I understood him exactly, and he understood me, yet over the years we talked very little. He never showed his own feelings.' For a while Foulkes had continued as a part-time player working full-time down the mine.

Towards the end of the 1953 season Johnny Carey was out of the side and Busby said to him one day: 'Would you like to do a job for me? I'd like you to take a look at an inside-left playing for Barnsley at Leicester.' Off went Carey, to return in a state of high excitement, considering himself to have made an important discovery. He quickly told Busby: 'This fellow is tremendous. We must have him!' Without evident concern Busby replied: 'Yes, that's the ninth good report I've had. I'd better go and have a look for myself.'

The player was Tommy Taylor, who like Byrne was to gain an international reputation with England almost overnight. With several clubs besides United chasing him, Barnsley put his fee at £30,000. There is no doubt whatever that Taylor, a naive, unsophisticated youngster, had no idea either of his own immense potential or where to take it. In the event, it was the personal magnetism of Busby that swayed him. It is almost incredible now, in times when players are negotiating a *share* of their transfer fee in the region of £12,000, that at no time in the discussion between Taylor and Busby was there any mention of what his wages would be. His only concern was that his mother and father should get tickets to watch him play. For four days before the deal went through Busby and Murphy stayed at a small hotel in Barnsley to make sure they did not miss their man. When at last Taylor agreed to sign, Busby managed to knock the price down by £1, the idea being to avoid Taylor being 'burdened' with a £30,000 fee, but the result was that there was more publicity and nonsense written than ever before.

When the young prodigy at last arrived at the railway station at Manchester he had his boots in brown paper under his arm. Johnny

Carey, who had gone to welcome him, spirited the parcel away and thus spoilt a picture which the milling photographers would have thrived upon. As a centre-forward Taylor had many qualities, but the most novel was his ability to make telling runs to the wings, outpacing full-backs and centre-half and creating gaps through the middle for his colleagues. In the air there have been few better. Ten years in advance he was playing in a style similar to Geoff Hurst of West Ham, who led the England attack in the 1966 World Cup triumph. But for Munich they might have played alongside each other.

In the seasons 1953–4 and 1954–5 United finished fourth and fifth in the League. The bombshell was about to burst. The spirit and competition within the club was now without parallel. As Foulkes recalled: 'No one could afford to step out of line or have a bad game. If you did there were two others waiting to jump into your shoes.' The average age of the side was 23. They were tagged 'Busby's Babes', but it was a misnomer, for their training and experience had made them, like Busby, old before their time, and they played with a maturity and assurance that had the whole of football agog.

Surprisingly, they had three lean years in the F.A. Cup. In 1954 they went out at the first attempt to Burnley 5—3; the following year 2—0 to Manchester City in the fourth round; and in 1956, the biggest shock of all, to Bristol Rovers 4—0 in the third round. Berry's wife and children were ill, Busby made last-minute arrangements for them to be taken care of, and Berry caught the midnight train, arriving in Bristol at 6 a.m. The young giants fell heavily that day.

In the League, however, there was no holding them. In mid-September Blackpool, Preston, Wolves and Charlton were setting the pace, United having taken only eight points from their first seven matches. Then they beat Preston 3—2, and on October 8, Wolves were mastered 4—3 at Old Trafford to put them level at the top with Blackpool and West Bromwich. Sunderland began to creep up, but United beat them 2—1 on December 3, and over Christmas resounding victories over West Bromwich by 4—1 and Charlton by 5—1 lifted them four points clear.

By the end of February, United had 44 points from 32 matches, Blackpool 38 from 31. On April 7, 1956, at Old Trafford, Blackpool made their last bid to stay in the race. They led 1—0 at half-time, but afterwards a penalty by Berry and a fine goal by Taylor gave United an even bigger margin. They finished the season a blistering 11 points ahead of Blackpool, an all-time record. In the Central League they were winners by five points, and again the club won the Youth Cup. In 10 years Busby's overall system had gained a grip on the English football scene never equalled or likely to be.

The only survivors from the team which won the Championship four years before were Berry and Byrne, and Byrne had been converted to full-back. The only changes in the side during the season were that Colman succeeded Whitefoot half-way through, and Greaves ousted Foulkes for a while at right back. The team was (3–3–4):

Wood

Foulkes (or Greaves)   Jones   Byrne

Colman   Whelan (or J. Blanchflower)   Edwards

Berry   Taylor   Viollet   Pegg

Only three of these had cost a fee—Wood, Berry and Taylor. It is perhaps here worth considering the controversial accusation often levelled against Busby—that he managed to sign so many of his young stars by tempting them with under-the-counter payments. There is the often told, apocryphal story of Joe Armstrong being encountered on a train one day by the scout from another club. Up on the luggage rack Armstrong had a small parcel, containing boots for a player. 'What have you got up there?' asked the other scout. 'Fivers,' said Joe.

The facts inevitably lead to suspicion. Mark Jones, United's massive young centre-half, stepped straight out of school into the car of Eric Taylor, manager of Sheffield Wednesday. The parents of David Pegg watched him play for England Schoolboys at Chesterfield with tickets provided by Sheffield Wednesday; on the Monday, Pegg was due to start his career at Hillsborough. But both Jones and Pegg finished up with United.

Edwards, Charlton and others were persuaded to follow this football Pied Piper when they had seemed destined for other clubs. What was the attraction? The circumstantial evidence for inducement is powerful. I admit myself to having supposed the obvious. If, after all, other clubs were offering financial bribes—and, in many cases, parents were demanding them—then surely it was likely that Busby was doing the same, only more successfully? Revelations from the club accounts in the eighties revealed this to have been so.

Yet looking at the other side of the coin it becomes increasingly clear that what *also* drew these boys to Old Trafford was the magnetism of the man himself and the dramatic, emotional appeal of the club, especially as events gathered momentum. It would be supposed that if he had given illegal money before a player signed, then he would have given more to them subsequently, disapproving so strongly as he did of the maximum wage. Yet whenever players went to him demanding more money, as Foulkes, then below the maximum, did on one occasion, his answer was always the same: 'You'll get your share.'

On tour in America in 1950, the players felt that they should be receiving more than their normal summer wage when they were helping to draw big attendances. Busby gave them a sharp dressing-down. 'I am not going to our hosts to point a pistol at their heads just because they are making more than they expected to.' I found nothing so emphatic as the comment of one of his players long since out of the game. Sitting in the comfort of his own home, yet compared with subsequent star players by no means well off, Johnny Berry told me: 'Busby would give you anything . . . that was legal. The only reason he was able to keep all those players contented, even when they were not in the first team and were getting nothing over the maximum, was that he had brought them up from boys and they worshipped him. If he had had the normal collection of players he would have never been able to keep them happy without the fiddles that were well known at other clubs, but which he'd have none of.'

Consider, too, the facts at the time of the 1948 semi-final, and the strike the following season, when Busby refused to budge in the face of demands. And if there were fiddles at Old Trafford would they really leave those facts in the books which in 1969 resulted in a

£7,000 fine by the Football League?

Paddy Crerand told the story of when he went to Busby to suggest that a certain player who was available on transfer would be a boon to the club. Even though the player was demanding a few thousand pounds on the side, Crerand thought that as Busby already had the reputation for such deals he might as well take advantage of it. Busby's answer was: 'That would not be fair.' There can be no doubt with the resources and influence available to him outside the club he could have had almost any player in the British Isles were he without principle. But long ago he had set down his attitude quite clearly: 'I have heard tales about what I am alleged to have done to sign player X, but I regard all such inferences as nothing but malicious nonsense, usually spread by other folk who have not been so fortunate in their quest for players. I have always played football on and off the field the way it should be played: that means I abide by the rules.' Time would demonstrate that Busby was a flawed genius, less than perfect for all his virtues. If Edwards, in the era of the maximum wage of £18, could die worth a five figure sum, it must be supposed that Busby had given him, shall we say, a precious Christmas present or two. Enquiries concluded some years after Busby's retirement did reveal payments by the club that breached regulations during his period of management. Whether they were made by him is doubtful, though knowing the extent of his control it is unlikely that he was completely unaware.

— 5 —

ELUSIVE TREBLE

The British are a conservative, placid race, which is probably why they have had few revolutions. It also means they progress only slowly. They are by nature suspicious of change, which is often wise because it prevents them from disposing of ways and institutions which have stood the test of time. But it also prevents them from grasping new ideas which could be beneficial. In 1953 the F.A. Year Book carried an article with the searching headline, *Has Floodlight Football a Future?* At that time the only First Division clubs with floodlights were Arsenal, Newcastle and Sunderland, and in the Second, Derby, Doncaster, Hull, Notts County and West Ham. In spite of the fact that the use of floodlights was increasing monthly throughout the rest of the world, the F.A.'s article remained highly suspicious of this new 'gadget'.

The following year, influenced by the formation of the South American Football Federation, the countries of Europe, *Britain excluded*, met to form the Union of European Football Associations (U.E.F.A.), with the hope of starting a European competition for national sides, such had been the success of the World Cup in Switzerland that summer. It was felt, however, that a competition for clubs would be more practicable, and the idea had rather lapsed when *L'Equipe*, the French daily sports newspaper, took a decisive hand in April 1955. The football editor Gabriel Hanot invited the delegates of 18 leading European clubs to a meeting in Paris. The following 16 attended: Honved, Budapest; Real Madrid; Anderlecht, Brussels; Chelsea, who were on the way to winning the League Championship; Rapide, Vienna; A.C. Milan; Hibernian, Edinburgh;

Partizan, Belgrade; Sporting, Lisbon; Djurgaarden, Stockholm; F.C. Saarbrucken, Austria; Servette, Geneva; Hollands-Sports, Amsterdam; Rot-Weiss, Essen; Stade Rheims; Bold-Klub, Copenhagen. They all signified their willingness to take part; U.E.F.A. were notified, F.I.F.A. gave its blessing, and the European Champion Clubs Cup had been born. In August the first draw was made.

At which point, enter the Football League. Chelsea were advised that their participation might interfere with their commitments in the League and were intimidated into withdrawal. Hibernian, Champions of Scotland, competed, reached the semi-final before losing to Rheims, and were the richer by £25,000. In the final in Paris, Real Madrid beat Rheims 4—3; the referee, Arthur Ellis, was English, but the match attracted little interest at home. There were better things to think about, though the F.A. Year Book did draw attention to 'two new competitions' and ventured to suggest that 'there is every reason to believe that they will meet with considerable success and will become part of the essential fabric of European football'. The other competition was the Fairs Cup (later UEFA Cup).

In 1956 Manchester United were League Champions, and therefore eligible for the Champions Cup. Again the Football League management committee advised their representative not to compete, but Busby would not be put off. 'After two World Cup failures prestige demanded that the continental challenge should be met, not avoided.' Confident that the club's reserve power—Charlton, Dawson, Scanlon, Bent, Goodwin, Blanchflower, McGuinness, Webster—was more than enough to meet any demands that the extra strain of the European Cup might put upon it, he persuaded his directors politely to decline the League's advice. The English foot was in the door.

In the preliminary round United were drawn against Anderlecht of Brussels. In the first leg Edwards was out of the side through injury; Blanchflower, brother of the Spurs captain, Danny, played a fine defensive role in his place. While there was still no score, Jones handled, and from the penalty-kick Mermans, the Anderlecht captain, hit the post, Foulkes clearing. The Colman made the first goal for Viollet, and Taylor scored a second. It was a useful start to a new venture.

None could have imagined just what United would do to Anderlecht in the return leg, played at Maine Road because the floodlights at Old Trafford were not yet ready. It had been raining heavily and the pitch was covered in pools of water, but United gave a bewitching display that brought a feast of 10 goals for the 43,635 spectators. Viollet scored four, Taylor three, Whelan two and Berry the other. The only forward not to score, Pegg, made at least five of the goals in a performance he was never to surpass.

In an attempt to explain such a score, some people tried to say that Anderlecht were not really first-class opposition, yet they had recently defeated Arsenal and were clearly an accomplished team. Mermans, their captain, said afterwards: 'Why don't they pick the whole of this side for England? The best teams of Hungary have never beaten us like this. Even after Manchester had scored six they still kept running as hard as at the start. It was fantastic.' Busby's view in retrospect was that 'it was the finest exhibition of teamwork I have ever seen from any team, club or international. It was as near perfect football as anyone could wish to see.'

In the next round in October, in front of crowd of 75,598 at Maine Road, United beat Borussia of Dortmund 3—2 in the first leg. Viollet put them two up in the first 35 minutes, and Burgsmuller made it 3—0 when he deflected in a shot from Pegg. Two defensive errors, one by Byrne, allowed Kapitulski and Preissler to put Borussia back in the game and create some doubt about the return leg.

Although Borussia had all but drawn level, they would have have lost more heavily but for a memorable display by their goalkeeper Kwiatkowski. When United went to Dortmund for the return in November, they found a frozen pitch and Tom Curry, the trainer, had to do some hasty conversion on their boots to make their studs shorter. In a grim defensive performance, in which Byrne and Jones excelled, United scraped through to the quarter-final with a goal-less draw.

At this stage United's next opponents were still undecided. Honved, the great Hungarian side containing five of the national team which had twice thrashed England three years before, had left Budapest before the Hungarian uprising, and were now indefinite tourists in the Western world. In their first leg against Bilbao of Spain they had lost by the odd goal in five. They could not return home for the second leg, and Brussels was chosen as the most suitable venue. Busby went to watch. Bilbao increased their lead with a quick goal, and with Honved's 'keeper Farago off the field injured and Czibor limping between the posts in his place, it seemed that the Hungarians were finished when Bilbao led 3—1 and 6—3 on aggregate with 10 minutes to go. Then in a storming finish Kocsis and Puskas scored to make it 6—5, but they could not quite gain a play-off. The Honved team was Farago; Rakoczi, Dudas; Bozsik, Banyai, Kotasz; Budai, Kocsis, Machos, Puskas, Czibor. Subsequently Puskas joined Real Madrid, and Kocsis and Czibor went to Barcelona, taking part in that sensational finish to the 1961 final when Barcelona just failed to overhaul Benfica.

So in January United flew to Bilbao for the first leg of their quarter-final. They had a wretched trip, via Bordeaux; Jones and Whelan were ill during the flight, Foulkes went to sleep with his feet on a lever, thereby turning off the heating so that everyone arrived shivering, and the plane made a nightmare landing at a deserted, snow-bound airport. Bilbao had been defeated only once at home in the last three years, and by half-time they were leading 3—0. United could have scored in the first minute but Viollet's shot stuck in the mud right on the goal-line. The ball was cleared, Jones slipped making an interception on the muddy, snow-spattered pitch, and Artiche raced on to score. However, in the space of eight minutes after half-time Taylor and Viollet made the score 3—2 and United seemed to have recovered. Not so, for Bilbao added two more with headers, and with only fives minutes to go their 5—2 lead looked an insuperable task for United in the second leg.

It was now that Liam (Bill) Whelan scored one of the outstanding solo goals in the history of the European Cup. Edwards, breaking up a Bilbao attack, found Whelan with a pass out to the right. Setting off on a diagonal run, the tall Whelan drove himself through the mud in a frenzy. One, two, three, four, five defenders were left behind as Busby, Murphy and the rest of the United party on the touchline watched spellbound. On and on went Whelan, finally hammering the ball past Carmelo in goal into the far top corner. This great goal gave United hope where a moment before there had been none. Two goals to recover at home was reasonable. Before they could leave for home the players had to sweep the snow off their plane, and they made a nerve-racking landing in bad weather at Jersey *en route*.

International sport is an unfailing cause of ill-will, wrote George Orwell, author of *1984*, but after Manchester United's visit to Bilbao they received the following letter:

> Under-Secretary of State
> Foreign Office
> London
> January 30th, 1957

Sir,

I am directed by Mr. Secretary Lloyd to state that you may be interested to know Her Majesty's Consul at Bilbao has reported on the excellent impression created by the football match held on January 16th between Manchester United and Bilbao Atletico. Her Majesty's Consul remarks on the great cordiality and good feeling on all sides which he believes has made a definite contribution to Anglo-Spanish relations. . . . As we all know only too well international sport can so often engender bad feeling instead of good. I believe on this occasion we have every reason to be well content at the conclusion of a British team's visit to a foreign country, and for this happy result the Manchester United representatives, players and non-players, who by their bearing and behaviour during an arduous visit proved themselves first-class 'unofficial ambassadors of Britain', must take their full share of the credit.

> I am,
> Sir,
> Your Obedient Servant

Although United might be conquering new fields in Europe, gaining prestige for themselves and English soccer, Busby was still busy looking ahead to the future. Never would he rest on his laurels. The same afternoon as the return leg against Bilbao, he watched his Youth side draw with Everton at Goodison Park on their way to the club's fifth successive victory in this competition. From Goodison he drove hurriedly to Maine Road.

Uribe, who had scored two of Bilbao's goals in the first leg, was now unfit, and the Spaniards brought in Etura, a wing-half, to bolster their defence, though they were still confident that no team could score the three goals United needed for victory. For some while it seemed they were right, for half-time had almost arrived without score. Then, as in so many matches for United and England, Edwards took a decisive hand. Driving through from mid-field, he had a fierce shot cleared off the line by Garay, only for Viollet to pounce and score from the rebound.

Still United seemed a long way from the semi-final in the second half, as the German referee, Albert Dusch, disallowed goals by Viollet and Whelan for off-side. With 20 minutes to go Taylor hit a post and followed up to score, but with five minutes left it was still 5—5 on aggregate. Taylor then made one of his characteristic runs down the right, leaving Garay trailing. Holding the ball till he was sure of the position, Taylor finally crossed it for Berry to hit the winner from close in. At their first attempt United were in the semi-final.

Although many of the continental teams were on a bonus of sometimes hundreds of pounds a man for these major European Cup games, all the United players received was an 'appearance fee' of £5 or £10. Busby's main comment after the Bilbao triumph was rather sour: 'The prestige brought to English football deserves something more than praise.' Bill Foulkes remembered this as, in his opinion, his own greatest game.

On the domestic front United were having another season in which they swept all before them, with the addition that this time they were going well in the F.A. Cup. Thus not only had they the objective of emulating the feat of Aston Villa in winning both Cup and League, in 1897—then a far simpler task than now—but of a unique and sensational treble, including the European Cup. In the League United were out in front for almost the whole way, headed only by Spurs for a brief period. In spite of the strain of two simultaneous cup competitions, they managed to maintain astonishing consistency in the League, and finished winners by eight points from Spurs, thus ensuring a second season in the European Cup.

In the F.A. Cup they had a scare in the third round—the point at which First and Second Division teams come into the competition—when they had to play away to Hartlepools. Leading 3—0, they eased off and allowed Hartlepools to draw level, and for a time the underdogs pressed hard for the winner that would have sent United's dreams tumbling. Then once again Whelan came to the rescue with the winning goal for 4—3.

In the next round United cruised home comfortably by five goals at Wrexham, but in the fifth round it required Edwards to come up for the only goal against Everton at Old Trafford. The quarter-final, against Bournemouth, provided the sort of set-back which could have wrecked United's prospects in all three competitions. Jones, such a dominating centre-half, was injured, and had to leave the field. At half-time Bournemouth were winning 1—0, but Berry saved the situation with two in the second half, the second a penalty after a shot by Viollet had been handled. Jones had pleaded at half-time to be allowed back on the pitch, in spite of a very painful knee, typical of the spirit in the side. Busby brought him back on, not on the wing, which was the accepted thing in such situations, but at centre-forward, Edwards having moved to centre-half. It was one of Busby's principles throughout his career that 'speed and power on the wings must be maintained at all times'. He retained this belief even when wingers became 'unfashionable'.

The problem for any other club might now have been critical, but the absence of Jones was hardly noticed. Up stepped Blanchflower from the reserves, to such good effect that Jones could not regain his place once he was fit again. Soon another potentially disastrous blow befell the team. Taylor cracked a small bone and had to miss the F.A. Cup semi-final against Birmingham City, losing finalists the previous year. Busby now played a shrewd move. Birmingham had a powerful but cumbersome centre-half, Trevor Smith. Busby decided to bring in Bobby Charlton for his first cup-tie, and switch Viollet to centre-forward, the idea being for him to lure Smith away from the middle with his nimble footwork, creating the space for the others to go through the middle.

Slight and pale, Viollet was more frail than any of the great Manchester United players then or in the years to follow, yet perhaps he came closer than any to the combined tactical awareness and technical virtuosity of the Hungarians, Bozsik and Hidekguti. Like Finney, he had the supreme ability to play in any forward or mid-field position. In United's first six European Cup games he scored nine goals. It was Murphy's opinion that, although not seriously injured at Munich, Viollet was never quite the same player again.

Against Birmingham, even with Viollet nursing a groin injury, Busby's plan worked to perfection. Goals by Berry and Charlton inside 13 minutes saw United through to Wembley. There were accusations of time-wasting by United: provided that this was done by skilful slowing of the game while the ball was in play, something they had soon learned from the continentals, Busby was in full approval.

United were now at Wembley again for the final, and the treble was becoming increasingly a possibility. The precocious achievements of Busby's young, almost mythological heroes was the talking point of millions. Those who never normally thought about football suddenly took notice. On the Monday following the semi-final victory at Hillsborough, Frank Coles, then sports editor of the *Daily Telegraph*, wrote:

> 'The reason for their surge of popularity is quite simple. Under the expert and fatherly guidance of Matt Busby, a happy band of young men have developed a team spirit and comradeship seldom equalled in any of our sports. They give all they have for the club, and in all circumstances they try to play football. . . . United were indeed superbly served by their three young inside-forwards, Whelan, Viollet and Charlton, not as attackers alone but by the unsparing, willing way they chased back to help whenever their defence was under pressure.'

Whelan, tall and with a shuffling run and hidden reserves of power, was developing into a superb player. Billy Behan, United's Irish scout, recalled: 'I remember travelling to London for the 1957 final, and talking to Matt. He said that Whelan and Charlton would prove to be the best inside-forwards in football.' Charlton at that stage was still not even a regular member of the side. Whelan was on one occasion involved in an unusual confrontation with Busby. Worried by one of those periods of self-doubt that affect all players at times, and with the Irish knack of speaking his mind, he went to Busby and said that he thought he should be dropped. Busby gave him a long hard look and replied: 'No one tells me who to put in my team and who to drop. I manage this side. If I keep you in it is because you are playing the way I want you to. Keep playing this way, and don't ever do this again.'

The draw for the European Cup semi-final lengthened the odds against the treble. United were paired with the winners of Real Madrid and Nice, while Red Star of Belgrade met Fiorentina in the other tie. Nice had beaten Glasgow Rangers 2—1 in a play-off, but then went down 6—2 on aggregate to Real, the holders. Busby went to watch the game in Nice, and returned home in a mood of mixed admiration and anxiety. Bobby Charlton recalled: 'Usually he would never talk too much about the great players in opposing teams, not wanting to frighten you. But now he couldn't contain himself. This player he had just seen, Di Stefano, had just about everything, it seemed, from what he told us.' Accustomed as he was to thinking in terms of great players, Busby realised that here was someone unique. 'In a lifetime in football I have not seen a better player,' he said; in Busby's private hall of fame his illustrious countryman Alex James had just been deposed.

Two weeks after defeating Birmingham, United set off optimistically for Madrid. Busby had some anxiety when Whelan developed a nose-bleed during training on the morning of the match, but he recovered. There was a further and bizarre complication when some Real officials arrived in the United dressing-room shortly before the kick-off, showed Busby a collection of photographs of their players, and then asked him for those of United. This was apparently a move designed to confirm that each team was playing only the correctly registered players! All Busby could do was to assure the Real deputation that they could inspect United's passports back at the hotel afterwards.

Early in the game Taylor missed the chance of putting United in front from a good position. Although little Colman was doing a fine job in shadowing Di Stefano—when everyone had expected Busby to give the job to Edwards—it was clear that Real's attack was superior. After a goal-less first half, inside-left Rial headed home from a cross by Gento. United's defence had relaxed when they expected a free-kick to be given against Foulkes; Leo Horn, the Dutch referee, allowed Real the advantage. A breathtaking run by Di Stefano, who dribbled past three men and then lobbed the ball over Wood and in off the post, having spotted that Wood had come too far off his line, put Real two up, and though Taylor got one back, a third by Mateos left United with a monumental task on the return leg. Busby said afterwards: 'It could have been 2—1 instead of 3—1 if our policy had been all-out defence, though I am not certain of that.'

When they came to Manchester it was discovered that Real, in the intervening fortnight, had pulled a fast one. Disturbed by the way in which Pegg had outpaced their right-back Becerril in the first leg, and remembering the way United had overhauled Bilbao, Real 'borrowed' a full-back, Torres, from Zaragoza. United protested without avail, for Real had conformed with the regulation by notifying U.E.F.A. of the inclusion within the regulation time-limit. Meanwhile Busby, fancying his side's chances would be improved by a soft ground, had ordered the groundsman to use the sprinklers liberally. Real turned up to inspect the pitch in the morning and saw it covered in pools. Immediately they threatened to call the game off if the sprinklers were not stopped.

Even at the height of nervous tension, just before the most important match his club had yet played, Busby still had time for others. At 4.30, three hours before the kick-off, he received a phone call from Don Revie, at that time merely an ex-player of Manchester City who had moved to Sunderland after helping City win the 1956 Cup Final. Could he see the match? 'Ask for me when you arrive,' said Busby, and put the phone down. When Revie arrived with little time to spare, there were two complimentary tickets waiting, plus tea-tickets. A small act epitomising a big club.

United, riding on a wave of false optimism after their victory over Bilbao, this time misjudged their opponents. 'The trouble was, I think, we never seriously considered the possibility of Real scoring. We looked on it once more as a matter of whether we could get three,' Charlton said. In the event, they suddenly found themselves 5—1 down on aggregate, Real stealing the initiative with goals by Kopa and Rial. Kopa had been signed from Rheims following the 1956 final. With such a lead it was inevitable that Real relaxed, and in the second half United scored twice through Taylor and Charlton.

Real went on to beat Fiorentina 2—0 in the final. The average age of their team was 28, that of United 21. As Busby said afterwards: 'It was a contest between two great teams—a mature side and a young side, and, of course, experience told. But our time will come.' Visions of the treble, however, were over.

—6—
ROBBERY

Before the 1957 F.A. Cup Final Matt Busby said: 'We shall not fail for the want of trying. Now that the strain of this hectic season is almost over, and while victory is our crowning ambition, I will be proud of my team come what may.' Little did he know what fate held in store.

This final will always be remembered not because Aston Villa won it, but because Manchester United lost it. Before the match everyone but supporters of Aston Villa believed that Manchester United, already League Champions for the second consecutive year, had only to stand up to win and achieve the double—last performed, ironically, by Villa themselves exactly 60 years before. But after only six minutes a violent and controversial charge by Villa's outside-left McParland fractured the cheek-bone of United's goalkeeper Ray Wood. Reduced to 10 men, United played valiantly for the remaining 84 minutes, but with substitutes then not allowed, they were at too much of a disadvantage. Villa, in danger of relegation at one time during the League programme, won 2—1 and thereby denied a special place in history to potentially the greatest club side the game had ever seen. Within a year seven of the United side were dead.

It had been a worrying time for Busby leading up to the final. Viollet was still troubled by the strained groin he had had when he played in the semi-final. Should Busby risk Viollet, or rely on the relatively inexperienced Charlton? Finally he made the only choice open to a manager before the introduction of substitutes: he chose the fit player, Charlton, then 19. Yet I wonder how many managers there are who have travelled 500 miles in order personally to tell a player he would not be selected. Such was the sympathetic consideration Matt Busby gave Viollet.

He had already given his word that he would attend the Football Writers' annual dinner two days before the final. He therefore travelled to London to see Tom Finney nominated Footballer of the Year, and returned overnight to Blackpool, where United were staying, even though the team were travelling down that morning to their London headquarters. 'I was the only man who should tell Viollet he was not playing,' Busby explained.

In addition to Viollet, there had been doubt during the last week about Blanchflower, who suffered a similar groin injury only seven days previously in a League match against Cardiff at Ninian Park. Normally this is an injury which, as in Viollet's case, can only be cured by prolonged rest. The position was doubly worrying because Jones had still not completely recovered from his knee injury. Yet Blanchflower made a remarkably quick recovery in only four days, and Busby was able to name the same side that had played in both games with Real Madrid:

Wood

Foulkes   Byrne

Colman   Blanchflower   Edwards

Berry   Whelan   Taylor   Charlton   Pegg

In considering the injury to Wood, it is worth noting the laws of the game in relation to charging. Then, as now, it is no different when charging the goal-keeper than any other opponent: the charge must be shoulder to shoulder, and the goal-keeper must be in possession of the ball. It is therefore obvious that to make fair charge it must be made from the side. But in almost all cases a goal-keeper is *facing* his opponent, so that a fair charge is impossible, unless the opponent first runs in a semi-circle to line himself up, during which time the 'keeper, if he is sensible, will have moved. Charging the 'keeper is thus out of the question in almost all circumstances, except when he comes down holding the ball having taken a centre sideways to his goal.

In 40 years I have only seen this done once legally, so as to score a goal by charging the 'keeper over the line—by Joe Baker of Arsenal for an England Under-23 team against Italy at Newcastle, and it took six minutes to restart the game, such was the Italians' indignation. While it would surely be sensible to abolish all charging of the 'keeper, referees in effect do so. This is not to say goalkeepers should not be challenged to make their clearance more difficult.

When McParland concussed Wood in the 1957 Cup Final there was no way possible for him at that moment to make a fair charge. McParland headed the ball towards Wood from out on the left; it bounced, and Wood took it safely into his chest, at least four yards off his line. He and McParland were then exactly face to face some 10 yards apart. But McParland rushed in, and as he reached Wood, took off from his right foot, turning his left shoulder in towards Wood's chest. Wood, rightly believing himself immune to a charge in such an unprovocative situation, had held his ground; and was now hit by the airborne McParland. The left side of McParland's head must have struck Wood's cheek-bone, giving it a depressed fracture. Wood's head jerked back under the impact, making his hair stand on end, and McParland spun off to Wood's right under his own momentum. It was one of the most unnecessary and regrettable actions I have ever seen on the football field. A pernicious foul.

Wood lay stunned, and was then taken away to the dressing room. McParland soon recovered, at least sufficiently well to score both Villa's goals in the second half. United, meanwhile, reorganised their side to such good effect that there was no score by half-time. Blanchflower went into goal, being an accomplished 'keeper in his spare time, and did wonders. Edwards moved to centre-half, and Whelan dropped back to wing-half, his performance making him for many the man of the match.

At half-time Ted Dalton, United's physiotherapist, went with Wood on to the strip of grass outside the stadium by the east entrance to the tunnel and the dressing rooms, and repeatedly threw a ball at him. The unhappy Wood, unable to judge anything on his right side and still badly dazed, missed most of them. A small boy, not recognising him or knowing the drama as 100,000 people waited inside to see if Wood would return for the second half, asked him if he would like to join a game with some friends round the corner.

It was clear that Wood was in no state to go back in goal, and Busby decided that he might just be of some nuisance value on the right wing, the only position where he could properly see what was happening on his 'good' left side. He was a sorry figure, and it was now that McParland scored his two goals. Yet there was even controversy surrounding the second of these. A shot by Myerscough hit the cross-bar above Blanchflower and rebounded to McParland, who hooked it into the net. Film of the match afterwards showed that as Myerscough shot, McParland was standing off-side beyond Whelan, and had only moved back into an on-side position as the ball rebounded.

Suddenly there was renewed hope for United, as Taylor, with not long to go, scored with a header. As a last gamble, Busby ordered Wood back into goal, allowing the team to re-form properly, but it was too late. Not only the treble but the double had proved a mirage. Villa had won the Cup for the seventh time. It was said that McParland got two goals and a goal-keeper, a view which Busby sadly endorsed. Foulkes later admitted that for the first and only time in his career 'I went after an opponent that day with the intention of nailing him'.

Busby was criticised at the banquet that night by a former England international for not having put Wood back into goal sooner. 'Well, maybe I should,' said Busby; then turning aside, he said scornfully to another guest about the man who had just been telling him his job: '*That* fellow, you had only to cough and he was off the field.' Foulkes, one of only four players that night who would return to Wembley the following year, recalled: 'It was typical of The Boss. He always took the long-term view. Winning a Cup Final was not worth jeopardising a player's career.'

The words of Eric Houghton, Villa's manager, quoted the following morning, are memorable for their inaccuracy as well as their apparent indifference to Wood's plight: 'There was nothing wrong in what McParland did. Wood was holding the ball and there was the chance that he could be charged over the line. [*In fact, Wood was four yards from the goal-line at the time.*] It was accidental that their

71

faces met. After all, a man doesn't use his face to hit another deliberately and his own cheek is badly bruised. I'm proud of him. Two
semi-final goals followed by two in the final is grand work.'

Arthur Oakley, the League president, was also depressingly conservative in his attitude to the handicap United had suffered: 'Many
will think that substitutes provide the answer to unfortunate hap-
penings like this. I'm not so sure. Don't forget, the cure sometimes
proves worse than the disease.' Such an attitude has only been surpassed in its irrelevance, I think, by the argument of Mr. Bob Lord,
the Burnley chairman, who at a League meeting some years later
expressed the opinion that substitutes would be a bad thing because
they would increase travelling expenses. The whole idea was
thought at the time to be in some way immoral, like boys' long hair
or girls' mini-skirts.

Wood's injury was the fifth in six years to mar the final. In 1952
Barnes of Arsenal twisted his knee. The following year Bell of Bolton
was injured. In 1955 Meadows of Manchester City, in the same spot
on the soft Wembley turf, twisted his knee in the same way as
Barnes, attempting to tackle the same player, Mitchell of Newcastle.
In 1956 Trautmann, Manchester City's keeper, played for some of
the game with a broken neck. His was one of only two sides to avoid
defeat. In the 1959 final Dwight of Nottingham Forest broke a leg,
though after his team was leading, and they were able to hold
against Luton, but in 1960 Blackburn lost a defender and went
down to Wolves.

Busby, pointing out that the law is unfairly weighed against the
goalkeeper—if he is fouled it is a free-kick, if he commits a foul it is
a penalty—said afterwards: 'If the manner of our defeat helps to
shake the dogmatic views so often expressed in connection with the
use of substitutes, that defeat will not have been entirely in vain.'

Nevertheless, it was a heartbreaking experience at the end of a
season in which Manchester United had reached for the moon. They
had played 57 competitive matches—42 League, 8 European Cup, 6
F.A. Cup and the Charity Shield. But they faced the future with a
depth of talent no club could match. As Busby remarked: 'With
youth teams talented enough to make a monopoly of the F.A. Youth

Cup for five years, there is no reason why Manchester United should not remain in the forefront of English and European soccer for at least another ten years.'

It was at the end of this season that Geoffrey Green, correspondent of *The Times*, asked Busby what he felt he had done for football and for Manchester United. Modestly, Busby replied: 'The time to judge me is when I am at the bottom.' That time was not far away.

A LEGEND MOURNED

While his young team were now a household word, their exploits had strengthened Busby's already substantial reputation. So it was perhaps not surprising that when, towards the end of 1957, he went to Paris for the European Cup draw he should be approached by a foreign club and asked whether he was interested in becoming their manager. British coaches were still much respected on the continent, even if British football had been going through a lean spell. Even so, nothing could have been more flattering than the offer now extended to Busby, for the club in question was . . . Real Madrid.

It was probable that Real, as much as Busby, had realised that even though they had won their semi-final meeting in the European Cup, to become champions twice in a row, time was on Manchester United's side. The lesson was obvious; if Busby could achieve success for United with players so young, he might do it for them. Di Stefano, Kopa and Gento would not last for ever.

Busby, however, knew instinctively that his job lay with his young players in Manchester. They too had a long way to go. Gratified by Real's offer, no doubt, he could not desert now. Though Europe had its attractions, the fabric of Old Trafford was almost woven into his soul. On the club's close-season tour in Germany he had said when interviewed: 'We would like to win the European Cup, of course. But above all I would like to win the English League Championship for the third year in succession. Herbert Chapman achieved this with Huddersfield and Arsenal, and it is the ultimate peak for any manager.'

Nothing would deflect him from his purpose of taking United to the top. In May, shortly after losing the Cup Final, he had rejected an offer of £65,000 for Tommy Taylor from Internazionale of Milan. He did not conceal the fact that the threat from wealthy foreign clubs worried him, with their ability to offer four or five times the wages to which he was restricted by out-of-date League regulations. 'I am convinced that the problem of under-the-counter payments and the exploitation of our best players can be completely solved only when the maximum wage is abolished and every man is paid what he is worth.' He would have to wait another four years for this to happen.

For a time at the start of the 1957–8 season it did not look as if United were worth quite so much as had been supposed. They lost 6—0 to Bolton, then 3—1 to Wolves, and were obviously struggling. Something had to be done.

By December 16, the team had suffered seven defeats, one more than in the whole of the previous season. One of the troubles was that Wood, though recovering from his broken cheek, had lost his confidence; Gaskell, a 17-year-old, was not yet ready. So on December 19, Busby paid the then world-record transfer fee of £25,000 for a goalkeeper, Harry Gregg of Doncaster Rovers. In November Gregg had given a marvellous performance in Northern Ireland's 3—2 win over England at Wembley, and now he came to Old Trafford at a time when a steadying influence was urgently needed for the young meteors.

True to style, Busby's reaction to a crisis was bold. For the Christmas game against Leicester out went Wood, Jones, Berry, Whelan and Pegg: in came Gregg, Blanchflower, Morgans, Charlton and Scanlon. Leicester were beaten 4—0. But the really remarkable fact, thinking of more modern times, was that not one of the five left out asked for a transfer.

In January things returned to normal, confidence spreading from Gregg right through the side. Charlton, then still little more than a boy, recalls: 'Harry seemed huge, and enormously strong. His handling was better than anything I had ever seen, and he gave us all a feeling that nothing could get by him.' While the League situation improved, Workington and Ipswich were beaten in the F.A. Cup, Shamrock and Dukla of Prague in the European Cup.

After the second leg against Dukla, United were held up in Prague by fog in London; their B.E.A. flight could not depart. Eventually they were able to get a flight to Amsterdam, continuing the journey by boat from the Hook, and then by train to London and Manchester, arriving weary and a day late. Always Busby was worried about the possibility of failing to be on time for Saturday's League match and subsequent embarrassment with the management committee. It was the experience in Prague that persuaded Walter Crickmer, the United secretary, to charter a private plane for the next round—against Red Star, Belgrade.

For the first leg at home to Red Star, who had a team of 11 internationals, Busby left out five capped players—Wood, Blanchflower, Whelan, Pegg and Berry. The Yugoslavs' famous 'keeper Beara made three tremendous first-half saves from Edwards, and at half-time Red Star were leading 1—0 through Tasic. In the second half, with Edwards mastering the brilliant Sekularac, United were even more on top, but goals by Charlton and Colman did not leave much to spare for the return in Belgrade.

On February 2 United went to Highbury for a League game which, for two reasons, those who saw it will never forget. If there was one thing that distinguished Busby's youthful champions it was that they had learned to change their pace; they now had the mark of a handful of great teams, that of being able to raise their game—suddenly, without warning, and to order, to get out of difficulty. This match against Arsenal saw them at the height of their powers.

Arsenal had just been humiliated in the F.A. Cup by Northampton, and 63,000 people packed into Highbury to see if their club could regain their prestige. Edwards soon hammered United into the lead, and in no time they were three up. Then they coasted along, saving themselves for Belgrade. Arsenal, taking their chance, drew level 3—3. United effortlessly accelerated and led 5—3, Taylor scoring the fifth from an impudent angle, and though Arsenal scored again for 5—4, morally they had been routed. Scanlon on United's left wing had been outstanding. From London the team flew straight to Belgrade, many of them never to return.

The side for the second leg against Red Star was the same as at Highbury: Gregg; Foulkes, Byrne; Colman, Jones, Edwards; Morgans, Charlton, Taylor, Viollet, Scanlon. Within 90 seconds Viollet had scored, pouncing on to a back pass. On the half-hour Charlton scored twice in two minutes, and at half-time United's 5—1 aggregate was daunting. But then Kostic beat Gregg from outside the penalty area two minutes after the restart; in the 55th minute a questionable penalty was given against Foulkes, taken by Tasic, and the Yugoslavs had suddenly scented blood.

The game now became excessively physical, with a profusion of fouls by either side as the Austrian referee lost his grip. With Gregg, Edwards and Morgans all injured, United had their backs to the wall. Moments from time Gregg, slithering out of the area, conceded a free-kick. Kostic scored to make it 3—3, but United were through to the semi-final for the second year running, 5—4 on aggregate.

United, conceding 36 free-kicks to Red Star's 11, were bitterly criticised the next morning in the Yugoslav press. Here was one of the earliest instances of the different interpretation of the laws, which increasingly was going to disrupt international soccer. The morning paper *Politika* said: 'Manchester were unsportsmanlike, and often unscrupulous. In the second half the British players felled opponents in an impermissible manner. Many times we asked ourselves where was the British fair play.'

That was one side of the picture. On the other hand the British press saw it rather differently. The *Daily Mail*: 'Referee Karl Kainer of Austria would have been howled off an English ground for his niggling anti-tackling phobia.' *Daily Express*: 'Almost unbearably exciting in the second half, a rough, tough tale of tempers and crazy decisions.' *Manchester Guardian*: 'It was a battle of wits and guts and rugged tackling.'

A story often to be repeated—inconsistent referee, rugged British tackling, emotional Central European or Latin response, especially when losing. It is however significant that Red Star's two most experienced players, right-half Mitic and goalkeeper Beara, were both of the same opinion: 'Manchester United are the better-qualified team for the semi-final.' Triumphant but a little sore, United took off for Munich and home, confident for Saturday's League encounter with the leaders, Wolves.

As their British European Airways Elizabethan G-ALZU A857 headed towards Munich on February 6, high over the Austrian Alps, the players relaxed. In the middle section of the plane Berry, Byrne and Blanchflower were playing cards. Gregg, who would usually have been with them, was dozing nearer the front, having wanted to play with Yugoslav currency while the others preferred English. Near Gregg, in another rear-facing seat, was Frank Taylor, correspondent of the *News Chronicle*, who would normally have been with his press colleagues, in the rear of the plane; but having an upset stomach, Taylor decided it would be more comfortable away from the tail. Such chance decisions by these two men probably saved their lives.

Also in the middle of the plane were Busby and Whalley—Busby weary and drawn, following a recent operation, Whalley only there because Murphy was in Cardiff to manage the Wales team in their World Cup tie with Israel. Geoffrey Green of *The Times* had also gone to Cardiff instead of Belgrade. When the plane landed at Munich, the runways grey strips on a white carpet of snow, the party left the plane for refreshments, then re-boarded, keeping their same seats. At 14.30 the plane accelerated down the runway, but half-way along shuddered to a halt. Captain Kenneth Rayment, the co-pilot, was at the controls, but Captain James Thain, the plane's skipper, had noticed a fluctuation in the boost pressure of one of the engines. The plane taxied back for a second attempt, but again there was fluctuation in the pressure, and again the brakes were applied. The plane returned to the terminal apron, and the party was asked to disembark once more while the fault was checked.

As they left the plane to splash back through the slush to the terminal building, Frank Taylor, who had been a wartime aircraft fitter, gave a glance at the wings to see if there was any ice. Even when there is no snow or ice on the ground, the fuel in a plane's wings, which cools far below the freezing point of water at 20,000 feet, will cause water vapour in the air to form ice on the wings when the plane has landed. But Taylor dismissed the idea, supposing that the ground crew knew their job.

After only a brief stay, too brief it seemed at the time, everyone was called to re-board again for a third attempt to leave for London. Back in the plane, Bobby Charlton fastened his seat-belt and looked at his watch: ten to three. There was a delay when it was discovered that one of the party was missing. Then Alf Clarke, of the *Manchester Evening Chronicle*, was seen hurrying across the tarmac. He had just sent his last despatch.

At 15.03, G-ALZU A857 once more rolled down the runway, accelerating till it reached 117 miles per hour. As when they had landed from Belgrade, Frank Taylor noticed that he could not see out of the window because of the slush thrown up by the wheels. Along on the flight-deck, Thain again noticed a surge in the boost control, and suddenly the air-speed indicator dropped from 117 m.p.h. to 105 m.p.h. Now he could see the end of the runway. Rayment, at the controls, shouted: 'We won't make it.' Frantically Thain tried to retract the undercarriage, but the plane would not lift. As they hurtled down the runway, Bill Whelan, Irish Catholic, said quietly: 'If anything happens, I'm ready.'

Frank Taylor turned in his seat, saw the perimeter fence, was then conscious of a blow behind the ear, and remembers no more. Busby, he later told Taylor, put his hand up as if to shield his face—then darkness. The plane roared on, crossed the landing lights, smashed through the perimeter fence, and after another 250 yards hit an unoccupied house standing in the line of the runway. The port wing was ripped off. The plane spun round and round, hit a wooden hut stored with oil and petrol, bounced into trees and finally came to rest, the undercarriage and the tail torn off. In barely one minute a great football team had been shattered; over half of them now lay dead, many other people, too.

In the cockpit Rayment was trapped in the crushed left side, but Thain and Rogers, the radio officer, both uninjured, climbed out of the wreckage and set to work with fire-extinguishers on the several small fires, for any moment the plane might explode. Harry Gregg emerged from the smouldering craft and, surprised to find himself alive, dived back inside to reappear with a tiny, unharmed baby, daughter of Vera Lukic, wife of the Yugoslav air attaché in London.

Again Gregg went back into the wreckage, and found Mrs. Lukic alive. Bill Foulkes, gathering consciousness, saw Thain tapping on the window beside him, and remembers thinking this was odd, because in front of him the fuselage had been torn away and Thain was close enough to touch him. Thain shouted at him to run for it, and with only one shoe on, Foulkes sprinted to the edge of the airfield where people were gathering. Then, seeing that the plane had not exploded, Foulkes rushed back to help with the rescue of those still alive.

He found Charlton and Viollet still strapped in their seats over 50 yards from the plane, unconscious. He thought they were dead. Nearby was Matt Busby, sitting in the snow, propping himself up on one arm, his ribs crushed, saying weakly: 'My chest.' Charlton soon regained consciousness, and came over to Busby. He recalled thinking 'how old and pale The Boss looked. I thought, "We're young and fit, but will he be strong enough to make it". It seemed somehow so unfair.' Soon an ambulance arrived and took Busby to hospital, Foulkes and Charlton with him. The driver went at a frightening speed, even in the snow, with Foulkes punching him on the head in a vain attempt to make him slow down.

Back at the scene of the crash, Peter Howard, a *Daily Mail* photographer, was doing valiant work to save the injured. Wood was trapped under one of the undercarriage wheels, Scanlon was pinned by one of the heavy baskets containing the kit; Frank Taylor, critically injured, was under a metal spar. The survivors all say no praise was too high for the selfless efforts of Howard.

Within 20 minutes all the injured were in the Rechts der Isar Hospital, the emergency procedure grimly efficient. Hovering between life and death were Matt Busby, his chest and foot crushed, his lung collapsed; Duncan Edwards, his thigh smashed, and kidneys punctured; Johnny Berry, in a deep coma with head injuries; Frank Taylor and Ken Rayment, the co-pilot, both with multiple injuries.

Dennis Viollet, Bobby Charlton, Albert Scanlon, Ken Morgans

and Ray Wood all had superficial injuries; Jackie Blanchflower had a fractured arm and pelvis. Mrs. Miklos, wife of the travel agent, would never walk again. Her husband was dead.

So, too, were seven members of the team: Roger Byrne, left-back, and his reserve, Geoff Bent; Eddie Colman, right-half; Mark Jones, centre-half; Bill Whelan, inside-right; Tommy Taylor, centre-forward; David Pegg, outside-left. For two weeks Duncan Edwards, the greatest of them all, fought against his terrible injuries, but in vain.

Eight journalists had perished: Alf Clarke, *Manchester Evening Chronicle*; Don Davies, 'Old International' of the *Manchester Guardian*; George Fellows, *Daily Herald*; Tom Jackson, *Manchester Evening News*; Archie Ledbrooke, *Daily Mirror*; Henry Rose, *Daily Express*; Frank Swift, *News of the World*, and former England goalkeeper; Eric Thompson, *Daily Mail*. The club had lost, in addition to its players, three officials: Walter Crickmer, secretary; Bert Whalley, coach; Tom Curry, trainer. Also dead were W. T. Cable, steward on the aircraft; B. P. Miklos, travel agent; and W. Satinoff, a supporter of the club and racehorse owner, while Rayment did not survive his injuries.

The four o'clock edition of the *Manchester Evening News* carried in the Stop Press the result of the 3.45 race at Wincanton: a normal day. A few minutes later the terrible news began to chatter over the teleprinter from Reuter. In *The Times* sports department I was watching awestruck as it appeared. Among the list of survivors in those first stricken, anxious hours was an unknown Andrew McDonald. Peter Howard and Bill Foulkes, when they telephoned Manchester as soon as possible to give the news of who was safe, had said that Frank Taylor had been pulled alive from the wreckage. But for many hours the official list did not include his name. In fearful anguish his wife tried to reassure herself, because although Andrew McDonald was given as a crew member, these were also the first names of her first son. Had they been taken in the turmoil from her husband's passport? In fact, Frank himself, in his state of shocked semi-consciousness, had given this as his name to the hospital staff.

All that evening and the following morning the appalling news was received by a stunned nation. In the streets in Manchester people cried. In the shops and factories and pubs there was a grief-stricken silence. The mood and sorrow of the country was best conveyed in the following tributes. The leader in the *News Chronicle* on the morning of February 7 said:

'Cutting out all the cant about sportsmen being ambassadors, it remains true that a team at this level of achievement plays a definite part in national prestige. It may be loved or castigated at home: abroad its triumphs and humiliations are looked upon nationally. Even those who have no interest in football must recognise that hundreds of millions of people, whose pleasure cuts right across the more formal frontiers of diplomacy, are today united in a sense of loss.'

'Silchester' of the *Manchester Guardian* wrote of Busby, in what all feared might be an obituary:

'Above all he recognised, in hitherto unparalleled numbers, fine players very early in their footballing lives. He wanted them so to think about the game that when a movement broke down, they spun a fresh one out of its fragments. Because he had no time for drilled footballers, the genius he discovered remained genius. His players were men in their own right, so that even youths such as Colman, Edwards and Whelan stood out as characters as well as fine players. . . . Even under strain they invested the playing of the game with something near indeed to glory in the imagination of hundreds of thousands who had never come within miles of Manchester. If their triumph has become a wreath it is one which will not fade in many memories.'

And H. E. Bates, the author famous for his war-time novels, wrote the following tribute for the F.A. Year Book:

'Late on a cold February afternoon, I was driving home from London when I suddenly saw, under the first lighted street lamps, one of those blue and yellow news placards that are designed so often to shock you into buying a newspaper you don't particularly want and that nine times out of ten, you would be just as well off without. 'Manchester United Air Crash" it said. My immediate reaction was, I confess, a mildly cynical one. The announcement seemed to me to belong to precisely the same category as "Winston Churchill in Car Crash"—the car crash almost invariably turning out to be nothing more than a tender argument between the starting handle of an ancient Austin Seven and the great man's Rolls somewhere in the region of Parliament Square. I am getting too old, I thought, to be caught by newspaper screamers.

At six o'clock, out of pure curiosity, I turned on my television set. As the news came on, the screen seemed to go black. The normally urbane voice of the announcer seemed to turn into a sledgehammer. My eyes went deathly cold and I sat listening with a frozen brain to that cruel and shocking list of casualties that was now to give the despised word Munich an even sadder meaning than it had acquired on a day before the war when a Prime Minister had come home to London, waving a pitiful piece of paper, and most of us knew that new calamities of war were inevitable.

Roger Byrne, Bill Whelan, Duncan Edwards, Tommy Taylor, David Pegg, Geoff Bent, Mark Jones, Eddie Colman—of Manchester United's flashing young giants hardly one had been out of his cradle at the time of the first Munich disaster. Probably not one of them had kicked a football in that year, on the eve of the war, when England had sent to Berlin 11 other giants to thrash the team representing Hitler's master race by six goals to three. By the time the war was over it was inevitable that the heroes of that resounding Berlin victory—men like Tommy Lawton, Raich Carter, Wilf Copping and Stan Cullis—were on the verge of slipping from the international football scene. A new race of giants had to be found to represent the country that had taught the rest of the world all that's best in the skill and beauty of soccer. And soon, as men like Carter, Drake, Lawton and Cullis turned their talents to the tutorship of new teams, we began to hear more and more of a man, up in Manchester, who appeared to be dedicated to the apparently revolutionary notion that you can make mature footballers out of boys in their 'teens.

To me that idea of Matt Busby's never seemed in the least bit extraordinary. There is nothing more true about football than that it is a young man's game. In youth the eyes have a fantastic swiftness; limbs are marvellously supple, with powers of recovery and resilience unknown later. The clay of young flesh is a beautifully plastic thing, that can be trained and shaped under skilled teaching in endless and remarkable ways. Not only in football has the principle of shaping extreme youth proved to be an excellent one. Who, 20 years ago, would have dreamed of swimmers of 13 and 14 representing their native countries and breaking world records? Today these things are commonplace.

Gradually, as the Busby principle of teaching was translated into reality, the names of the top students began to emerge. We began to hear of players representing Manchester United in the First Division at the age of 17. Presently we were to see the greatest of all the Busby prodigies, Duncan Edwards, an appealing giant of a boy, representing England when barely 18, striding the Wembley pitch like a mature colossus, gaining the first of his 19 international caps, under each of which he increased in stature so much that at 21 he was not only a veteran but England's future captain. If I selected Duncan Edwards as the most compelling of all the young Manchester men who will now never play football again it is because he always seemed to me the epitome of all that was best in skill and character in the team that became known— and very foolishly, I think—as the "Busby Babes".

I have always disliked that cheap journalistic label and I have a fancy that most of the players may have done so too. There was certainly nothing of a babe about Edwards. A more mature young man, great in both physical strength and artistry, never walked on that treacherous and difficult turf at Wembley to play for his country. You could almost say the same of that excellent and cultured full-back Roger Byrne, who gained 33 England caps; of the energetic and enthusiastic Tommy Taylor; and of Pegg, Colman and Jones, all of whom, like Duncan Edwards had been schoolboy stars; of Whelan, who also appeared for his native Ireland,

and Bent, who travelled to Belgrade as reserve. Footballers, George Bernard Shaw once said, have their brains in their feet, but I have always had a sneaking notion that Matt Busby liked to be sure that his young men had a few brains in their heads too.

But what these young prodigies possessed above all, I think, was class. It is an attribute not easy to define, but when Manchester United were beaten in the 1957 Cup Final by an Aston Villa team playing very robust but not very good football, it was pure class that made them, I think, as admirable in defeat as they had so often been in victory. . . . Whether the same degree of class will ever be seen again in the United colours it is too early to tell; but one thing is certain. If it never returns it will not be the fault of Matt Busby, the tutor, still happily with us, or of the young men to whom, so very early in life, he taught the beauties of our national game and who, having acquired fame in youth, set such an adult example before they were so prematurely and tragically taken from the field.'

———

The relatives of the survivors quickly flew out to Munich. Busby, near to death, was in an oxygen tent, his breathing assisted by a tracheotomy because of his collapsed left lung. Twice he received the last rites from a Roman Catholic priest. On the second day after the crash, Sandy, his son, said: 'Dad spoke to Mother and seemed to be trying to cheer her up.' For Jean Busby it was an ordeal more than for most. She had known many of the dead players almost as well as Matt. Not long before, he had written: 'With Jean I have had the two most priceless assets any man can hope to possess—a good wife and a happy home life.'

After five days an artificial kidney was flown from Freiburg for Edwards, whose huge physical resources alone had kept him alive. When I visited the Rechts der Isar Hospital in 1969 Dr. Hans Schaefer, one of the surgeons who fought night and day to save those most gravely injured, told me: 'I do not think anyone other than this young man, with his remarkable physique, could have survived so long. His resistance made us all admire him. At one point we believed him saved.' They showed me the dusty, yellowed file that contained the story of Duncan's fight for his life—three lines on graph paper, green, red and blue that daily recorded his pulse, temperature and blood pressure. For 15 days the lines inched forward, each day another victory, but at 01.12 on February 21, 1958, they came to a halt. For Duncan no game was ever lost till the final whistle went, but this was one even he could not win. Slowly, in spite of the kidney machine, his body had been poisoned. Yet even had he won, it is doubtful if he would have played again, so badly broken was his thigh.

Duncan played his first game in the First Division at the age of 15 years and 8 months—the youngest ever—against Cardiff on Easter Monday, 1953. He was the youngest ever to play for England, at 17 years and 8 months, against Scotland at Wembley in 1955, when England won 7—2. He had nine schoolboy caps, three youth championship medals, two First Division Championship medals, an F.A. Cup losers' medal, and 19 full England caps. In the 1956-7 season he played 95 games for Manchester United, England and the British Army, and in the last, for England against Czechoslovakia, he was the best player on the field, scoring two goals. Let us leave the last word to the late Willy Meisl, of Austria, respected critic throughout the world: 'Duncan Edwards was a *nonpareil*. I have never seen a better half-back, a more complete footballer, a young man who had everything from physique to understanding, from ball control to fighting spirit. He could win a match alone, and won many . . . for me he was much greater than the great John Charles, because with all his calmness there was also a fierce fighting streak in Duncan, the most lovable boy ever to run on to a football field.'

Edwards' death brought United's toll to eight players, three of them pillars of the England team. With Byrne, Edwards and Taylor, it is quite possible that England instead of Brazil might have won the World Cup in Sweden that summer. They were, in the event, the only team against whom Brazil failed to score. Walter Winterbottom, the England manager, was one of many to weep that day in February.

Six days later, on February 27, a German Catholic priest finally broke the news to Busby which the hospital had kept from him. Dr. Georg Maurer, the chief surgeon, to whom Busby owed his life, had insisted that he must not be told. 'We planned to keep it from him for at least another month,' said Dr. Maurer. For three weeks Busby's wife had withheld the dreadful facts. To his repeated questions, Jean had given the same white lies: that Duncan was ill but making progress, even when he had already died. When Jean visited him on this evening, Busby whispered: 'I know about Duncan. I want to know everything.'

A doctor was fetched, and they tried to change the subject. But Busby would not be put off, and eventually the doctor agreed; slowly he spoke to his wife. Later Jean said: 'Matt remembered everyone on the plane. Every time he mentioned the name of one of the dead players, I just nodded. It seemed as if it would never end.'

For almost three days afterwards, Dr. Maurer recalled, Busby hardly spoke or ate. It was because he had feared the awful truth which he now knew, that he had previously prayed for death. He recalled: 'It was at a time when I gradually became aware that some of my boys must have been killed. I did not know for certain. I just knew something dreadful had happened. I was in that tent, barely alive myself. Twice I had been given the last rites. I just wanted to stay inside the tent and die there, rather than come out and learn the truth. So I prayed for the end to come quickly.'

Now, as Busby fought not with his injuries but his new grief, the arguments over the crash continued elsewhere. Both the Germans and B.E.A. held inquiries. The Germans said that ice on the wings was the main cause; B.E.A. considered that it may have been slush on the runway. Some people questioned why Captain Rayment, who had died from his injuries, was at the controls rather than Captain Thain, the senior officer. But both were of equal rank, and Rayment had 3,000 hours' experience in Elizabethans, twice the amount of Thain.

The Germans established that 16 other aircraft had successfully taken off on February 6, and that all had been de-iced. At the time United's plane attempted to take off there was a car out on the runway measuring slush, which was not considered beyond the safety limit. The Germans pointed out that there was five millimetres of ice measured on the wings of the crashed plane. This would mean it could not lift off the runway in under 2,300 yards, beyond the perimeter fence. But the measurement was not taken until six hours after the crash, by which time there had been a further fall of snow.*

* See Appendix III

The engines were tested later and judged not to have been responsible for the failure to lift. Yet how reliable can any such test be after a plane has crashed at 110 miles an hour? If they were not faulty, then what was the change in note and pressure that Thain detected on all three runs? One Air Correspondent at the time stated: 'The surge could have been the engines racing, which could be caused by the propeller slipping and acting as a *brake*. Normally an Elizabethan should be able to climb fully loaded on one engine.' But these were not questions that concerned Busby.

The anguish in his mind was whether there had been anything that he, as the man in charge of the party, could have done to avert the disaster. I would totally refute this. At no point was there any evidence upon which he could even begin to form a judgement that would lead him to query the course of action. It is suggested that the time spent back at the terminal buildings between the second and third attempts was too short for a satisfactory check on the apparent fault. What, to the layman, is a satisfactory time? Half an hour? One hour? If you tried to solve this kind of arbitrary problem, you would never board a plane at all.

It took Busby 10 weeks to recover sufficiently to return to England. As he lay there it was not the pain in his broken body but the torment of his soul that must have hurt the most. As he said later: 'So many times I have asked myself whether there was anything I could do, or ought to have done, to stop that plane. But you saw how it was. We went back to the terminal buildings, and everything seemed to have been checked. It would have been as pointless for me to ask the pilot if everything was in order, as for him to ask me whether I had picked the best team for Manchester United.'

It was one of the mercies of this tragic day for British sport that the architect of the glory which had been shattered had himself survived. For the moment, the harrowing job of rebuilding would have to wait. One of the first to arrive at the Rechts der Isar after the crash had been Jimmy Murphy, whom fate had diverted to Cardiff on the fateful day. Feebly, Busby said to him: 'Keep things going for me.' Of course. But how?

ABOVE Busby in his Liverpool playing days. 'There were times when I
thought I had no future in the game'.

ABOVE Busby, the embryo coach and manager, showing a youngster in 1937 the style that made him an international wing half.

BELOW The FA Cup-winning team, 1948. Back (l/r): Petheridge (dir), Gibson (dir), Whittaker (dir), MacLean (dir), Hardman (dir). Middle: Crickmer (sec), Anderson, Chiltern, Crompton, Aston, Cockburn, Warner. Front: Delaney, Morris, Carey, Busby, Rowley, Pearson, Mitten.

ABOVE Roger Byrne leads out United for the ill-fated Cup final of 1957
against Aston Villa ahead of Berry, Blanchflower, Wood, Foulkes,
Charlton, Taylor, Whelan, Edwards, Coleman (hidden) and Pegg.

BELOW The Red Star goalkeeper punches clear from Viollet (left) and
Taylor in the European quarter-final in Belgrade prior to the Munich
crash in which Taylor and eight others died.

BELOW Busby hovers between life and death in an oxygen tent, his lung punctured. The last rites had been administered.

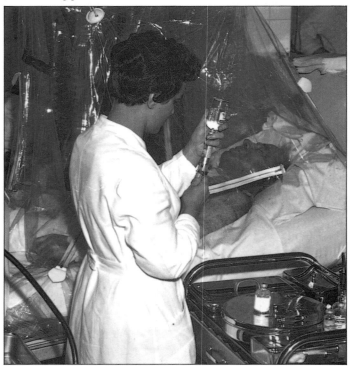

LEFT Busby briefing the team in Belgrade before the match, one of the last photographs to be taken before the fatal return journey. Back (l/r): Whalley (coach), Blanchflower, Edwards, Colman, Jones. Middle: Taylor, Viollet, Wood, Curry (trainer). Front: Morgan, Charlton, Foulkes.

BELOW Needing crutches for his broken legs, Busby thanks Professor Georg Maurer on his release from the Rechts der Isar Hospital.

LEFT The team that won the second of consecutive Championships in 1957. Back (l/r): Webster (not on plane), McGuinness (n.o.p.), Blanchflower (injured), Docherty (n.o.p.), Coleman (died). Middle: Curry (trainer, died), Foulkes, Charlton, Goodwin (n.o.p.), Wood (injured), Whelan (died), Jones (died), Edwards (died), Inglis (trainer, n.o.p.). Front: Viollet (injured), Berry (injured), Busby (criticially injured), Byrne (died), Murphy (Ass. Manager, n.o.p.), Taylor (died), Pegg (died).

BELOW A convalescent Busby watches United lose to Bolton.

LEFT Busby with survivors of the crash and new players leave for a friendly match in Munich. Left (t/b) Scanlon, Cope, Dawson, Foulkes, McGuinness, Charlton, Quixall, Shields. Right: Gregg, —, Brennan, Viollet, Carolan, Bradley, Goodwin.

ABOVE Dennis, the King, beats Banks in the 1963 Cup victory.

BELOW Dennis Law holds the League Championship trophy of 1965.
Back (l/r): Connelly, Brennan, Best, Crerand. Front: Dunne, Ryan,
Herd, Law, Foulkes, Stiles.

ABOVE Law (8) characteristically heads a goal in the victory over West Ham that secures the 1967 Championship. Moore (6) is grounded.

BELOW And Crerand gets another.

ABOVE The squad that fulfilled the dream of winning the European Cup. Back (l/r): Foulkes, Aston, Rimmer, Stepney, Gowling, Herd. Middle: Sadler, Dunne, Brennan, Crerand, Best, Burns, Crompton (trainer). Front: Ryan, Stiles, Law, Charlton, Kidd, Fitzpatrick.

BELOW Stepney and Charlton parade the cup after beating Benfica at Wembley.

ABOVE A lifetimes' fulfilment – Busby is mobbed by players and the crowd.

ABOVE A gentle knight. Sir Matt outside Buckingham Palace with Sheena Gibson (daughter), Lady Jean and son Sandy.

BELOW Freedom of the City of Manchester for the man who bought freedom of thought to the game.

Above George Best – legendary figure of Old Trafford's greatest years.

Below Manager of the Year with the Footballer of the Year, 1968.

ABOVE Benevolent eye. Busby announces retirement after 23 years as
manager.

ABOVE The players stand for a minutes' silence as a sign of respect for
Busby and his legacy to the game.

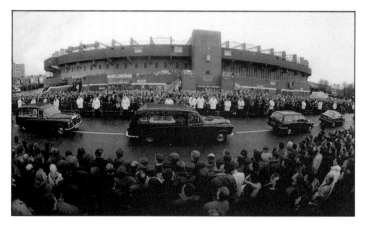

ABOVE AND RIGHT The people
of Manchester mourn the man
who will be forever associated
with their city.

—8—

TIDE OF EMOTION

How to form a new team around two men? This was the nightmare that confronted Jimmy Murphy, as together with Harry Gregg and Bill Foulkes he sat in the German express train taking them back to England. When, in 1949, the plane carrying Torino Football Club had crashed into a hill at Superga, killing all on board, not only was it the end of Torino's domination of football in Italy but the start of the decline of the national team, which had won the World Cup in 1934 and 1938. Now, almost 10 years later, neither Torino nor Italy had really recovered from the disaster. What could Murphy hope to do to repair his shattered club?

Although some players had been saved, and most of these had only minor injuries, would they ever be the same again? And how would these two men with him react once they returned to Old Trafford, with all its memories of their dead colleagues? It was an overwhelming burden that Murphy shouldered as they made their way home.

For Foulkes the journey was agony. 'Every time the train braked I was in a cold sweat,' he said. 'It was all I could do not to scream, and at every stop I wanted to get off. When we arrived at Dover I could hardly face the rest of the journey. I had to insist that Jimmy kept the window of the train open. I could hardly eat or sleep for the next month, and I lost over a stone. One or two things were comforting. Real Madrid offered us all a free holiday in Spain, to help us recover. I think one or two of the fellows took them up on this.'

When they arrived in London the two players were in such a state of nervousness that Murphy hired a taxi for the rest of the journey back to Manchester. The strain on his own nerves was intense, for not only was he trying to care for the survivors and their dependants, but there were the immediate demands of Manchester United's fixtures. At the time of the crash the club was, as the year before, involved in two Cup competitions as well as the League. Their next League fixture, against Wolves on February 8, had been postponed to give them breathing space. Yet time was one thing, finding the players another. And always Murphy was haunted by the knowledge that he should have been on that plane, sitting next to Busby instead of coach Bert Whalley, who was dead.

After Wales had beaten Israel at Cardiff in their World Cup play-off, Murphy had arrived back in Manchester the following afternoon, taking a taxi from the station. 'United must have a chance in the European Cup this year,' the cab driver had said cheerfully. At that moment United's chances already lay in ruins.

When he reached Old Trafford, Murphy had hurried up to his office. There were things to be attended to in time for the important clash with Wolves two days later. As his secretary, Alma George, called out to him, he did not detect the anxiety in her voice. A little abruptly he asked for a cup of tea. 'Mr. Murphy,' she said, near to tears, 'haven't you heard? The United plane crashed at Munich.' It was four o'clock. By four the next morning Murphy had drunk a bottle of whisky without knowing it, as frantically he tried to piece together the facts of the tragedy from different sources.

Before the crash, United's playing strength was such that they were fielding six internationals in the Central League reserves. Now 17 players, including the dead, were out of action, 10 of them internationals. The only two clubs to come forward with genuine offers of assistance as opposed to sympathy were Liverpool and Nottingham Forest. Tom Williams, Liverpool's chairman, telephoned Murphy to ask if any of his club's lesser-known players would be of use. Bob Lord of Burnley, with his insensitive bluntness, said that United could not expect other clubs to weaken their staffs just to help them out of trouble. This was not quite as bad as the club which telephoned Murphy at the height of the crisis to offer him the post of manager—

seemingly a deliberate attempt to undermine United's survival.

It crossed Murphy's mind that the Hungarians, Puskas, Czibor and Kocsis, were still unattached in Western Europe, and there was correspondence with the Hungarian Football Association in Budapest about their possible 'transfer'. Yet this would have been contrary to the whole tradition established at Old Trafford by Busby, quite apart from the problem of work permits, so Murphy decided to confine his search to England.

He happened to know that Ernie Taylor, an ageing but shrewd inside-forward, was anxious to leave Blackpool and get back to his native north-east. Taylor was the player who had been the arch schemer in two Cup Finals—for Newcastle against Blackpool in 1951, making the winning goal, and then for Blackpool against Bolton in 1953. Professionals will all tell you that it was Taylor as much as Stanley Matthews who hauled Blackpool from the brink of defeat to win 4—3 in injury time and give Matthews his long-awaited winners' medal. It only needed a short talk with Taylor for Murphy to convince him that United's needs were a challenge to his still considerable skills. Taylor signed, for an £8,000 fee—now Murphy had a team of three.

Stan Crowther made it four. Crowther, a blond and tough wing-half, had been in the Villa side which destroyed United's dreams of the double in the Cup Final the year before. He would supply some of the bone to back the brain of little Taylor. United's F.A. Cup fifth-round tie against Sheffield Wednesday was put back from February 15 to the following Wednesday evening, February 19. The programme for that night was printed with eleven all too eloquent blanks in the United team. When Murphy sat down finally to pick the side he burst into tears. He had a line-up of two survivors, Gregg and Foulkes; two makeshift signings, Taylor and Crowther; and seven almost unknown youngsters, several straight from the third team. As Crowther had appeared for Villa in the third round when they were beaten by Stoke, he had to get special dispensation from the Football Association to play, which was only granted on the afternoon of the match. The teams that night were:

UNITED

Gregg

Foulkes   Cope   Greaves

Goodwin   E. Taylor   Crowther

Webster   Dawson   M. Pearson   Brennan

Finney   Froggatt   Shiner   Wilkinson

O'Donnell   Quixall   Kay

Johnson   Swan   Martin

Ryalls

WEDNESDAY

Most people had expected Manchester United to withdraw from the Cup. How could the club possibly go on? Yet the next few weeks were to show that Matt Busby had created something far larger than even he had planned. The people of Manchester, hiding their wounded hearts behind a surge of pride, helped to sweep their team onwards in a huge tide of emotion. Nothing quite like it had been seen before. Wherever United played, the gates were closed. The support that roared out was as relentless as a storm at sea. The stakes were suddenly far greater than the game itself. Harold Hardman, the chairman, expressed the feelings of all at Old Trafford, indeed all of Manchester, when he wrote in the programme that night against Sheffield Wednesday: 'Although we mourn our dead, and grieve for our wounded, we believe that our great days are not done. The road back may be long and hard, but with the memory of those who died at Munich, of their stirring achievements and wonderful sportsmanship ever with us, Manchester United will rise again.'

Brave words, but who would have believed that the prophecy would be so immediately given substance. Poor Sheffield Wednesday had little stomach for the fight that night, the will of the whole country, it must have seemed, stacked against them. They were beaten 3—0, young Shay Brennan scoring two. Phoenix-like, United were still alive.

In the League, not surprisingly, United slumped. They won only one more match, against Sunderland, drew five and lost eight to finish the season in ninth position—their lowest since Busby arrived at Old Trafford 13 years before. But in the Cup their luck miraculously held, partly due to some superb performances by the young Charlton, the brilliance of Gregg in goal, and the way Ernie Taylor marshalled the youngsters around him in mid-field.

In the quarter-final West Bromwich, considered by some the Cup favourites, were beaten in a replay after a 2—2 draw at the Hawthorns in which United led 2—1. In the replay at Old Trafford there was barely a minute left when Taylor sent Charlton away down the right wing. In a fantastic run he left two defenders stranded as he went down the line, beat two more cutting in, then slid the ball wide of the goalkeeper, Sanders, for Webster, the 18-year-old Wales outside-right, to put the ball in an empty net. With a goal at the very end of 180 pulsating minutes United were through to the semi-final. The programme carried a tribute to Edwards, speaking of 'his awe-inspiring demonstration of seeming invincibility, coupled with a joy of living that infected his comrades whenever and wherever the going was tough'. Without him, this makeshift United had defeated one of the most distinguished sides of the fifties. It was: Sanders; Howe, S. Williams; Dudley, Kennedy, Barlow; Whitehouse, Robson, Allen, Kevan, Horrobin.

A few days later Dr. Georg Maurer, the German surgeon, arrived in Manchester as a guest of United, so that he might see the club whose injured he had so skilfully tended. With him be brought a tape-recorded message from Busby for the Old Trafford crowd at the next home game. Also, on a slip of paper, in a painfully weak hand, were the names and addresses of the bereaved whom Busby had asked if he would visit on his behalf. In Munich, Busby was now fit enough to get up for a few minutes each day, but was still weak and in great pain.

Before the semi-final of the Cup against Fulham, Johnny Haynes said in an interview: 'It may make us the villains of Villa Park, but we are determined to smash Manchester United. We'll pull no punches.' If this sounded bold, it was probably more an admission that Fulham knew they had more to beat than a football team; they had to give a slap in the face to the sentimental hopes of a whole nation. Fulham were very nearly true to their word. They had the better of the first half, but then Jim Langley, their left-back, was injured and two goals by Charlton gave United a replay at Old Trafford; a last-minute save by Macedo in the Fulham goal, turning a shot by Charlton on to the bar, had prevented United snatching a dramatic winner.

If Macedo had been Fulham's hero in the first meeting, he was now a sorry figure in the replay at Highbury, sadly at fault on more than one occasion as United stormed to a 5—3 victory. A header by Dawson from Webster's cross put United ahead; Stevens, put through by Haynes, made it 1—1. A shot through Macedo's hands by Dawson again put United in front: again Fulham hung on with a goal from Chamberlain. Brennan and Dawson scored for 4—2, Dwight reduced the lead to 4—3, and Fulham were then unlucky to have a goal disallowed which would have put them level once more. Finally Charlton left Macedo groping with a thunderbolt of a drive, the kind which crowds all over Europe were to come to expect from him. Unbelievably, United were in the final for the second year running.

Before the final, against Bolton Wanderers, Jackie Blanchflower and Charlton were walking down the street in Manchester when Blanchflower spotted in the Stop Press of the evening paper that Charlton had just won his first cap for England, against Scotland at Hampden—the start of an international career which was to make him Britain's best-known player throughout the world since Matthews. He celebrated his selection with a glorious goal from Finney's centre in a 4—0 win. The England team was: Hopkinson; Howe, Langley; Clayton, Wright, Slater; Douglas, Charlton, Kevan, Haynes, Finney.

Again and again, when talking to those who knew Busby for many years, they will say, reflecting upon what helped to make him such an outstanding manager, 'He was a great family man. Whenever you went to Old Trafford they were always there: Jean, Sheena and Sandy.'

For a time Sandy, his son, had ambitions of following in his father's steps as a player, but they were unfulfilled. Sheena, his daughter, married a footballer on the United staff, Don Gibson. The time came when Busby, as a matter of diplomacy, felt that it would be better if his son-in-law was with a different club, and he was happily transferred to Sheffield Wednesday.

Now, as the family tried to re-form their life, Matt and Jean drew great strength from each other. Wives of United players repeatedly tell of the interest, support and understanding they had from Jean Busby, who was to them what Matt was to his players—a source of comfort, advice, assurance and help. Yet in addition Jean was, in the opinion of one who knows the family well, 'the iron fist behind this gentle man'. She it was who now willed him back to health; who with a deep feminine pride was determined that he should recover to continue in the job that belonged to him, jealous perhaps of anyone taking over what he had so painstakingly created.

By the time the final approached Busby was fit enough to leave the Rechts der Isar Hospital, where he received a heart-felt farewell, and made his way overland with Jean back to England. There was talk of his being able to lead the team out from the tunnel at Wembley, but he was still walking only with great pain, and besides, he felt that honour belonged to the man who had breathed faith and willpower into the players who had so astonishingly achieved the impossible—Jimmy Murphy. So Busby took up a place behind Murphy on the touchline.

At the tactical discussion beforehand, Busby came in to congratulate the young team, and to give them a pep-talk. But as he looked around at these youthful faces, whom he had only known as boys but now suddenly carried the responsibility of men, he was overcome with emotion and, tailing off, had to leave the room.

Murphy, omitting Morgans, McGuinness, Pearson and Brennan, had selected the following side (3–3–4):

Gregg

Foulkes   Cope   Greaves

Goodwin   Taylor   Crowther

Dawson   Charlton   Viollet   Webster

The game could not have begun more badly for United. After only three minutes Lofthouse, Bolton's experienced war-horse of a centre-forward, swept home a centre, and suddenly all the emotional strength seemed to drain away from United. Now they were seen for what they were: young, uncertain, too heavily taxed by the strain there had been upon them in recent weeks. This was the anticlimax. 'We played the final at Third Division level,' recalled Foulkes. 'I think our supporters, more than we, had got the club to the final.'

Maybe Crowther might have prevented the first goal. There was briefly a surge of hope as a shot by Charlton beat Hopkinson in goal, but it bounced back off a post and into his arms, and for the second year running a controversial goal settled the issue. Gregg parried a shot from Stevens, cousin of Duncan Edwards, and as he caught it at the second attempt, Lofthouse charged him in the back from behind, the impact 'bursting' the ball from his grasp and over the line. This obvious foul is now included in a F.I.F.A. documentary film as an example of illegal charging of the goal-keeper, but the goal was allowed and Bolton were winners. Their team was: Hopkinson; Hartle, Banks; Hennin, Higgins, Edwards; Birch, Stevens, Lofthouse, Parry, Holden.

There remained the semi-final of the European Cup. For the first leg at Old Trafford, England rather uncharitably obliged United to play without Charlton, who shot the winner from 30 yards in the friendly match against Portugal at Wembley. If the reason for not releasing him was the imminence of the World Cup finals in Sweden it was seen in retrospect as rather irrelevant when, after a poor game in the following match against Yugoslavia in Belgrade, he was left out against Russia in Moscow, and was ignored for the whole of the World Cup tournament. Even without him, United managed to beat A.C. Milan 2—1 with goals from Viollet and Taylor, but were hustled out in the return 4—0.

What did the future hold? Busby was back in the seat of authority at Old Trafford, but it would be many months before he could give himself wholly to the sad business of trying to repair his life's work. And if he did make a full recovery physically, had he the emotional strength? Those who doubted did not know the man. Searching ahead through the mists of sadness he said: 'Deep down the sorrow is there all the time. You never really rid yourself of it. It becomes part of you. You might be alone, and it all comes back to you, like a kind of roundabout, and you weep. . . . The first time was when I went back to the ground at Old Trafford after the accident. I just looked at the empty field, and in all my life I have never felt such a terrible vacuum. And so I cried, and afterwards I felt better for the tears, and because I had forced myself to go back there. It was something I'd done, something I'd conquered. The first rung of the ladder. . . .'

BUYING TIME

If the Football League were misguided to advise Chelsea and Manchester United not to compete in the European Cup in its first two years—advice Busby had sensibly disregarded—in the autumn of 1958 they carried bureaucratic intervention to its nadir. As a gesture of sympathy and admiration, U.E.F.A. invited Manchester United to compete again in the competition, in addition to Wolves, the new League Champions. The League management promptly ruled that United were ineligible, and should not take part.

United successfully appealed to the Football Association. Not content to let the matter rest, the League then forced a meeting of the joint F.A./League consultative committee on September 5, and this reverted to the original decision that United were ineligible. In a battle of power politics the F.A. had allowed themselves to be out-manoeuvred, having stated in a letter to United on July 5 that there was 'no objection to your club taking part'. And charity, they say, begins at home.

If the football authorities did not seem to appreciate what Busby and United had done for English soccer in the last three seasons, at least the effort did not go unnoticed elsewhere. In June Busby received the C.B.E., which must have been a filip to his summer convalescence in Switzerland. His own restoration was no less uncertain that that of his club.

Yet if will-power could succeed he was half-way there. In spite of appeals from his directors to cushion himself from further strain, he had this compulsive drive to defy misfortune. At one stage during his recovery Jean Busby said: 'He has this tremendous determination to get better, completely better again. Steadily he has forced himself to walk without his crutches, then without a stick. In spite of the pain, he has managed to get his foot back into a football boot, so that he can tap a ball around again. He says he will be running round the track training with the team again soon. If he says this, he will do it.' This couple, both children of miners, had known misfortune before in their 28 years of marriage. Four times they had lost a son soon after birth, while Jean had endured ill-health for much of the time during Matt's playing days.

With the death of Tom Curry, the trainer, in the crash, Jack Crompton, United's former goal-keeper, had been invited to return to Old Trafford from Luton, where he had a similar post. Luton had readily agreed. Crompton, among a handful of people, knew just what Busby went through in his fight back to fitness. 'He would walk down the corridor to his office with his arms outstretched using the walls instead of his sticks to steady himself. Once he started driving again, the pain from his back made even a drive as far as Blackpool a labour. He would change position fifty times on the way.'

Crompton soon found himself absorbing the philosophy which Busby instilled into his coaching staff. 'You can only threaten and bully players so far,' he told Crompton, 'then they'll turn against you. You have to study their different points of character, and try to get at them through these, to take them with you rather than push them. It is no use insisting on something as a matter of principle, merely to satisfy your own ego, because although you may succeed for a time this way, eventually you will have lost that player, and in that way you are not helping the club but hindering it.' One player with whom Busby could not establish an affinity was Colin Webster, the young Wales winger, and after a while he was transferred to Swansea.

No one knew better than Busby that something had to be done to strengthen the playing staff, in spite of the performances that had carried them to the Cup Final after the crash. The man he had his eye on was an inside-forward who five years previously played for England at 19, but was now something of a forgotten man—Albert

Quixall, a member of the Sheffield Wednesday side beaten in that first emotional cup-tie after Munich. Busby approached Wednesday, who at first were reluctant to part with Quixall; then, in the middle of September, they said that he was available.

On September 18 the morning papers all carried the news that Busby was travelling to Sheffield to sign the former 'golden boy', so called on account of his blond hair and precocious talents. No fee had been discussed with Wednesday, and when Busby arrived he was asked how much United were prepared to pay. He replied that he only bought a player who had a price on him. So Wednesday named it—a staggering, in those days, £45,000. The record at that time was £35,000 for Jackie Sewell (Notts County to Sheffield Wednesday) and Cliff Jones (Swansea to Spurs).

The fee took Busby's breath away, and his answer was no. He then remembered that the press, radio and television were assembled outside waiting to record the event. What should he tell them? 'Tell them you can't afford it,' joked Wednesday's manager Eric Taylor. Busby departed, announcing that the matter had been shelved, but before midnight he had telephoned to say that United accepted the price and they would return the next day. He duly returned with a United director, Louis Edwards, and signed the cheque. 'Don't you want to speak to the player *first*?' asked Eric Taylor. In his haste to restore United's prestige, Busby, the master of detail, had overlooked the point of whether Quixall would want to come to Old Trafford. A short conversation soon confirmed that he would.

The next day Quixall was in the team against Spurs at Old Trafford, Ernie Taylor being dropped. The papers reported that Quixall 'hardly looked the golden boy'. It took him some while to settle and by the end of October United had gone seven matches without a win. The tide turned on December 1, when United won 4—0 at Birmingham. Quixall and Charlton for the first time found real understanding; one report stated that 'the quality of the team would not have disgraced the pre-Munich side'.

Taylor had been transferred to Sunderland, Crowther went to Chelsea; into the side came McGuinness at half-back and Warren Bradley, an England amateur from Bishop Auckland, at outside-right. United hit a winning streak and took 23 points from their next 12 matches. Through the autumn it had been Arsenal and Spurs who made the running, Spurs beating Everton 10—4. Then Wolves took four points off Portsmouth at Christmas to go top, while United, with four points off Villa, moved into fourth place. Wolves then twice lost to Chelsea, and by February Wolves and Arsenal had 41 points, United 40. Arsenal now began to slip, and United finished the season six points behind Wolves in second place.

There was one black spot on their record. In January they were beaten 3—0 by Norwich in the third round of the cup, Norwich going on to defeat Cardiff, Spurs and Sheffield United to reach the semi-final, where they lost to Luton, who in turn lost to Nottingham Forest in the Final. Norwich's scorers against United were Bly (2) and Crossan. Busby told their manager, Archie Macaulay, his old wartime colleague: 'You beat us by football. Your men played the correct game, whereas mine didn't change their tactics when it was obvious that short-passing wouldn't pay.'

It was the fifth time since Busby became manager that United had finished runner-up, in addition to their three championships. He said: 'All I was hoping for was a reasonably safe place in the First Division until we get things sorted out. These boys have played better than I dared hope. But a lot still has to be done. It will take years to try and build up again.'

If Busby had momentarily forgotten his principles over the Quixall transfer, an incident during the 1959 close season illustrates, better than any in 25 years, his consideration for his players and their families. The club was going on a summer tour and the point had arrived where it was obviously necessary that they should fly once more. The flight was only a short one, to Rotterdam, but for Busby, as for the other survivors of the crash, Gregg, Foulkes, Charlton, and Viollet, it was an ordeal.

Talking about the flight later, Busby said: 'I swore I'd never fly again. Once, at the hospital, I remember, they wheeled me out on a stretcher into the sunshine on a verandah. As we left the door, I had a sensation of flying again. Before I knew it I was screaming. . . . But there was something that made my fly again. One of the teachings of the Catholic faith, as I understand it, is that your life is in the hands of God . . . that when your time comes you must be ready and prepared, for you will surely not miss it. Why then, I asked myself, was I avoiding the air? Was I so uncertain of my trust in God? So I flew again. It was only a short hop, but it was long enough. Every second of that flight was an endless torture. Along the runway I actually relived the whole crash.'

When the party arrived at their hotel in town they went as usual straight to their rooms to rest before having a meal. Jack Crompton, the trainer, was lying reading on his bed a little while later when in came Bill Foulkes. 'I've just been on the phone to my wife,' he said. 'I told her that we'd arrived safely, and she said, "I know." I asked her what she meant, and she said, "The Boss has already been on the phone to let me know."' He had already 'phoned the wives of the survivors to say that all was well.

———

Later the same summer, George Sturrup, the London agent for Real Madrid who had business interests in Spain, was coming out of the Fenix Hotel in Madrid, where most visiting teams usually stay, when he was surprised to bump into Matt Busby. 'What are you doing here?' asked Sturrup. 'I've come to visit Real, to ask if they would consider helping us. I'd like them to come to play us in a friendly match, to help get the crowds back and maintain the interest, now that we're no longer involved in the European Cup,' said Busby, his voice tired and care-worn.

It so happened that Sturrup was just on the point of going to see Santiago Bernabeu, Real's president, so Busby went with him. 'I'm afraid we may not be able to offer you the money you want,' Busby told Bernabeu, whose club, after winning the European Cup five times in a row, were asking £10,000 guarantee for friendly matches. 'Never mind,' said Bernabeu, 'how many matches do you want us to play. Two? Three? Just pay us what you can afford.' Seldom can one club have shown another such generosity, yet Busby has always had this ability to gain affection and admiration for Manchester United. Real duly came to Old Trafford, and tore United apart with football which none will forget.

For a while in the early autumn of 1959 it looked as if United might be going to have a good season. They beat Chelsea 6—3 at Stamford Bridge, but then followed successive defeats by Spurs, Manchester City and Preston, with one one goal scored and 12 against. Something had to be done about the defence, and in October Busby made a bid for Eric Caldow, the Rangers and Scotland full-back. Caldow thought about the move for a few days, then turned it down. Joining United was no longer quite the attraction it had been.

One of the sad aspects of the situation then was that some of those players who had survived the crash had lost their edge. While Gregg, Foulkes, Charlton and Viollet remained the foundation of the team, Morgans and Scanlon were never quite as effective. Morgans followed Webster to Swansea, and Scanlon, who in that memorable game against Arsenal just before Munich had looked one of the best wingers in the world, departed to Newcastle. The side was short of stability at the back and the old flair, Charlton apart, in attack.

In the seasons 1959–60 and 1960–1 United finished seventh both times—solid enough, but unspectacular. In the Cup they went out to Sheffield Wednesday both times, 1—0 and 7—2 (after a 1—1 draw). Busby had said it would take time to regain their former status, but the situation was made the more difficult by a new development in the game. As Busby wrote with telling foresight in the 1960 edition of the *International Football Book*, published by Souvenir Press:

'Without wishing to belittle the achievements of any club, I feel certain methods of attaining success have influenced British football too much, and in the wrong direction. I am thinking of the power game. Results are achieved by placing tremendous emphasis on speed, power and physical fitness. Such teams now have many imitators. We are breeding a number of teams whose outlook seems to be that pace, punch and fitness are all that is required to win all the honours in the game. They forget that, without pure skills, these virtues count for precisely nothing. The imitators do not realise that Wolves, for instance, needed some-

thing more than that to get their good results. I should like to see
the honours in England won by a pure footballing side, the sort of
team that concentrates on ball skills above all else. Such a team
could inspire the other 91 clubs. But for the air disaster, I like to
feel that others would now by copying Manchester United, to the
benefit of the whole League.'

Such a team was, in fact, just round the corner—the marvellously
fluent Spurs team which, inspired by Blanchflower, White and
Mackay, was to achieve in 1961 the double which had eluded United. Yet whatever he thought of the power game, Busby, like anyone
else, was to some extent bound by expediency, and in January 1960
he bought Maurice Setters, a wing-half, from West Bromwich for
£30,000. This was forced upon him by the unfortunate injury to
Wilf McGuinness, who broke his leg having already established
himself as an international of some promise, gaining caps against
Ireland and Mexico. Setters was the England Under-23 captain: fearless, ferocious in the tackle, above all a superb competitor. Because
sometimes he used his great strength to excess, his by no means
inconsiderable skill tended to be overlooked.

Setters played his first game for United against Birmingham, helping them to win 2—1. At one stage he chested the ball down in the
penalty area and dribbled clear. Afterwards Busby told him: 'Look,
we don't want to play around in the box—get it away'—enough to
make Setters realise he had not been bought for his refinement.

He and Busby had their disagreements. After one game against
West Ham, Setters was leathering into his colleague afterwards—
never one to hold back his feelings—and Busby told him abruptly:
'Shut your mouth.' But an hour or two later he came up to him and
said: 'Don't worry, there's no need for us to fall out, you know.' Like
other players who had been at Old Trafford and then moved on, Setters said it was only later that he realised just what a fine manager
Busby was. 'There were times,' he recalls, 'when I would have
demanded more from the players, would have talked to them more,
when things just didn't seem to be happening. But later you realised
that his handling of men was tremendous. He somehow managed to

achieve things without talking.'

In April 1960 there was an example of Busby's shrewd judgement of players. United played a friendly match against Shamrock Rovers in Ireland, losing 2—3, the little Irish left-back having a fine match. Busby stayed on to see Shamrock play Shelbourne on the Sunday, and although this time the full-back was handicapped by a badly injured hand early in the game, Busby had seen enough to say after-wards: 'He'll make the grade.' It was Tony Dunne, and the £6,000 he cost United must have been one of their best-ever bargains.

The next move was to buy Noel Cantwell, a tall and dominating left-back from West Ham for £29,000; with two new full-backs, Foulkes could concentrate on centre-half, where his strength in the air was invaluable and his lack of speed was less exposed. In July Busby bought David Herd, son of his old Manchester City col-league, from Arsenal for £40,000, to add punch to a flagging attack. The way should now have been open for United to reassert them-selves, but things became worse, not better. In 1961–2 the top scor-er was Herd with 14 goals, the lowest by the club's top marksman since the war, and United finished 15th in the League, the lowest since 1938–9, when they were 14th.

There was some consolation in the Cup, in which they beat Bolton, Arsenal, Sheffield Wednesday and Preston before meeting Spurs, the holders, in the semi-final at Hillsborough. Since achieving the Double, Spurs had acquired Jimmy Greaves from Milan for £100,000, and now he struck a decisive blow before United knew what had happened. The game had barely begun when Danny Blanchflower chipped a ball down the middle; Bobby Smith, Spurs' centre-forward, back-headed it straight on, and there was Greaves going through, clear of everyone, to steer the ball home unerringly. At wing-half United had two inexperienced youngsters, Stiles and Lawton, and they were run into the ground by the wiles of Blanch-flower and White, Spurs finally winning 3—1. Attempting to kick the Tottenham pair, they found themselves kicking thin air.

The semi-final stage, anyone will tell you, is the worst at which to lose—far worse than the final, in which you have had at least the satisfaction of appearing at Wembley and gaining a losers' medal. In

the semi-final defeat does not bear thinking about, but it was to happen to United four times in five consecutive semi-finals from 1962.
Here again, Busby always demonstrated his unique capacity for lifting his side when they were down, for making virtue out of misfortune. Cantwell, later manager of Coventry, recalled: 'Those nights at
the banquet after we had been knocked out in the semi-final were
somehow even better than if we had won. Matt would make a
speech early in the evening, say how pleased he was, how well we'd
done, what an achievement it was to get so far, and before you knew,
you were feeling pleased too. Everyone would be there, from the
woman who washed the kit to the chairman, and there was this
wonderful feeling of being a great club and defeat suddenly being
unimportant. Matt would say, "We're going to have a splendid
night"—and we would. I just don't know how he did it. If I were
ever manager in the semi-final and we lost, I know I couldn't.'

Busby was particularly optimistic after the Spurs semi-final.
'Although we were defeated,' he said, 'I knew this was a turning
point. The signs were there that with this team at last we could
achieve something again.'

Not long after United had lost to Spurs an incident in Italy made
headlines in the British papers. Denis Law, who had been transferred
from Manchester City to Torino in 1961 for £100,000, was taken
off the field by the manager for allegedly not trying during a 2—0
defeat by Naples. Law was suspended from the first team and heavily
fined. There had been trouble throughout his time with Torino,
when he was hounded by gossip photographers as a result of some
skylarking with his colleague Joe Baker (who had come from Hibernian, spoke with a Scots accent, but played for England).

The affair had subsided, when suddenly one day Busby had an
unexpected phone call. It was George Sturrup, Real Madrid's agent
in London. He had had a call from Emil Oesterricher, the technical
director of Torino and previously manager of Real Madrid. Oesterricher told Sturrup that he was fed up with both Law and Baker and
wanted to transfer them; did a British club want them? Sturrup
immediately rang Busby. 'I've heard of two players available, who I
think might interest you,' he said. 'Oh, who?' asked Busby casually.

'Joe Baker,' said Sturrup, to see Busby's reaction, which was that he did not think Baker would fit into their plans at that time. And who was the other? 'Denis Law,' answered Sturrup, smiling to himself. There was almost an explosion at the other end. 'Don't open your mouth or move till I get to your house. I'll be there on the first train,' gasped Busby, putting on his hat and coat almost as he put the phone down. Within a few hours he was at Sturrup's house in South London, and from there they immediately made plans to meet Torino officials.

Denis Law, a slightly built Scot with fair hair, was then the most exciting thing in football—a player of razor-sharp reflexes, who could strike for goal at close quarters around the penalty area as fast as a rattlesnake's head. He could beat the most powerful centre-halves in the air with an astonishing leap for one so comparatively small, and he was as brave as a wounded elephant. You could say that he was priceless, but the combination of his volatile temperament and the discipline which exists in Italian clubs proved too combustible for comfort.

On May 3 there was a secret meeting with Torino in Amsterdam, where Real Madrid were playing Benfica in the European Cup final, and the basis of agreement was reached. On May 22 Busby, Harold Hardman and Louis Edwards travelled to Italy for further talks, but the next day they walked out of their meeting with Torino, Busby announcing that Law would not be joining United. The Torino president had tried to impose new terms on the transfer, and the United trio returned to England.

On June 20 the negotiations were reopened by Gigi Peronace, agent for a number of leading clubs in Italy, who had taken Greaves to Milan. Finally, on July 12, Law became a Manchester United player for £115,000, and the chase for the most expensive player in English soccer—at that time—was over. Busby had first seen Law as a boy playing for Huddersfield's youth team in 1957, and had tried then unsuccessfully to sign him for £10,000. So frail was Law when he first arrived from Scotland that some said he would never make a professional player. Yet he became one of the greatest in the game's history, and the sad thing was that he never had the chance to appear on the most important stage of all, the World Cup finals.

Yet though Law was an instant individual success, scoring 23 goals in his first League season, 1962–3, United's £300,000 team still did not click. For the first time since he took over, Busby was faced with the possibility of relegation. Now his equanimity was really to be tested, but not for one moment did he panic or falter in his conviction that all would be well, that there was nothing basically wrong with the way the team was playing. Bill Foulkes recalled: 'He never lost his sense of humour. Always he reassured us by saying, "The wheel will turn."'

In January, just when things were at their blackest, and he might have himself been despondent, he took Jack Crompton, the trainer, on one side. 'What are you worrying about?' Busby asked him. 'I'm not,' replied Crompton, who had never been more worried in his life. 'Yes, you are. But are we doing enough in our training, in your opinion?' Like any leader Busby knows that to inspire confidence you must show confidence in your subordinates. 'Yes, I think so,' replied Crompton truthfully. 'So do I,' said Busby. 'Now for heaven's sake stop worrying, and go and take your wife out for dinner at the club's expense this Saturday. Enjoy yourself, and let things take their course. We shall be all right.' With so much to lose this was a remarkable statement of faith.

Busby expected everyone to have the same faith, and was annoyed at the whispering campaign which began to gather force about whether he would be able to accept life in the Second Division. David Meek, correspondent of the *Manchester Evening News*, went to Harold Hardman, the chairman, solely with the intention of scotching the rumours of a divided camp. Busby was cross, suspecting that Meek was trying to get the chairman to make a slip of the tongue, and told him so. This sensitivity to journalistic comment was less personal resentment than a protective instinct for the club.

In the third round of the Cup in January, United put five goals past their former colleague Ray Wood, now with Huddersfield. Maurice Setters recalled that afterwards Busby said quite emphatically that they would win the Cup. This is the sort of thing that many managers tell a harassed team in January, and a hardened professional like Setters would not easily be convinced by such optimism. 'Yet it was not bravado,' Setters recalled, 'he really meant it. It was a rational, deliberate statement, and although I didn't take him seriously at the time, a day or two later I thought, "My God, he's right!"'

United proceeded to beat Aston Villa (1—0), Chelsea (2—1), Coventry (3—1), and, in the semi-final, Southampton (1—0), Law scoring the goal that took them to Wembley to meet Leicester City. By the time the final arrived they had escaped relegation, finishing three points ahead of Manchester City, who went down with Leyton Orient. The irony of Law crossing the city via Turin was not lost on City supporters.

United had at last begun to fully exploit Law's genius, it seemed, following Busby's decision to buy, on February 3, a 'middle-aged' wing-half for £43,000—a Catholic Scot like himself, Paddy Crerand of Celtic. By a strange coincidence, Crerand was probably the nearest replica as a player in the modern game to Busby himself: a superb striker of the ball, with a brilliant eye for angles and timing, the skill to play the game at his own pace, a shuffling, ungainly run, and a mature influence on the rest of the side. He was a sound buy.

Yet of the three sides that Busby had taken to Wembley—the remodelled side in '48, the home-grown teams of '57 and '58, and now this team assembled largely with a cheque book—the chances of the present side were the least optimistic. My much admired colleague Bob Williams, then northern sports editor of the *Daily Telegraph*, wrote before the final:

'Many think he [Busby] has failed for the want of a little healthy intolerance to make the third side match up to the first two, who were undoubtedly more dedicated to team-work and pure soccer. The 1963 team have never found team-work easy, but they have frequently shown a flair for the big occasion, and thereon depends their hope of victory on Saturday. Six of United's side, excluding Gregg, cost large fees, and it is open to question whether any of them has lived up to his previous reputation. Denis Law has done so in the sense that he has won matches virtually single-handed from time to time, but he has failed to draw the response from the team that United must have hoped for when they paid Torino £115,000 for him.

Quixall, their first big purchase, has been burdened ever since with the invidious £45,000 price label, Setters retains the dashing style that persuaded United to pay West Bromwich £30,000 for him, without becoming consistent or looking mature. Cantwell cost £29,000 and has not held a regular place even as club captain. Herd (£40,000) from Arsenal has shown signs of loss of confidence in a line dominated by individuality. The most recent arrival, Crerand from Celtic, was regarded by many as the best wing-half in Europe not long ago, and United's £50,000 may yet have been well spent. Crerand is technically best equipped of all to hold United together, but, like Law, has not consistently shown his best form at club level.

The one star player to have come through the junior sides is Charlton, who at a tender age came to bloom after Munich, but despite having more than 40 England caps, has gone back rather than forward in the last season or two, and appears to have lost the fearsome shooting power on which he built his reputation. No one, indeed, is in great form for United and no manager can have had more to worry him in the weeks preceding the final than Busby. His team were cleared of relegation worries last Saturday, and even against the weakest side in the First Division were not, apparently, impressive. But, far from black despair, there is always an optimistic disregard for the past at Old Trafford. Individual brilliance and the sense of occasion have won cups before, and Manchester United know very well that, if their last shred of prestige is not to slip from them, they must do so again.'

I am sorry to say that my faith was not so strong, and in my preview of the final in the *Sunday Telegraph* I tipped Leicester to win on account of their method and blend, which had been impressive throughout the season. The teams at Wembley lined up as follows (3–3–4):

UNITED
Gaskell
Dunne   Foulkes   Cantwell
Crerand   Quixall   Setters
Giles   Herd   Law   Charlton

Stringfellow   Gibson   Keyworth   Riley
Appleton   Cross   McLintock
Norman   King   Sjoberg
Banks
LEICESTER

For the first quarter of an hour Leicester's method gave them the edge; Gaskell and Cantwell were in difficulties in the United defence on several occasions, and Gibson might have scored. But the individual ability of Law and Quixall, with their rapid square passing in midfield, was beginning to give Leicester problems; Cross, McLintock and Appleton, Leicester's mid-field trio, were able to spend less and less time on attack, and the game slowly turned United's way. With half an hour gone, Law scored the goal that gave them the platform from which to launch an hour's display that did much to erase the memory of a season's ignominy.

Taking a pass from Crerand from the left, Law hooked the ball past Banks with such force that the effort threw him to the ground. A few minutes later Law dribbled clean through the whole defence and past Banks, only to see his final shot scrambled clear. Herd scored the second early in the second half, knocking in the rebound after Banks had been unable to hold a drive by Charlton. Now United cruised imperiously towards victory, until 10 minutes from the end a fearless diving header by Keyworth, taken off Dunne's toe, gave Leicester hope. United's answer was an immediate rally, Law hammering a header against a post with the power of a shot, and with a few minutes to go Herd got the third when Banks, with half an eye on Law, failed to hold a high centre from Giles.

United were back in European competition—the comparatively new Cup Winners' Cup—after an interval of five years. Busby said boldly: 'Individually, we have nothing to fear from continental opposition.' Yet this was the opposition for which he yearned, because it was the continentals, in his opinion, who played football as it should be played, on the ground. In England, he observed, because of the demands of the League competition, the proper way of scoring goals 'had become submerged in the general panic'—the panic to which he would never be a party.

—10—
THE LAST CHANCE?

If Busby's comment about the way the rest of the League was going sounded perhaps a trifle superior, he had good cause not to be worried about the future of his own forward line and its ability to score goals. He had up his sleeve a youngster who was going to surpass anything that even Old Trafford had seen before, a kind of Garrincha and Matthews rolled into one, with the appropriate name of Best. Two years previously Bob Bishop, United's Northern Ireland scout, had been in touch to tell Busby: 'I think I've found a genius.' Busby needed little time to agree, and directed the coaching staff: 'On no account change the boy's style. Let him develop naturally.' For George Best was, as they say, a natural.

There was not much of him at 15. When United invited him for a fortnight's training in the summer of 1961 he was so shy and uncomfortable that after 24 hours he and his companion Eric McMordie—later an inside-forward for Middlesbrough and Ireland—caught the boat back to Belfast. His father promptly phoned Busby, who assured him that he felt George had a fine future. The young Best was returned to Manchester in no time, more or less on the end of his father's boot.

The next two years Best spent training and playing with United's third team. Then, on Friday, September 13, 1963, this wisp of a youth who was just beginning to feel at home in the club, went to look at Saturday's team sheet, only to find his name missing; nor was it among the Central League side. Then he saw it—at the bottom of the first team: reserve. He was not to know that he had already been selected, but Busby, anxious not to let him worry, put down Moir even though Moir was unfit; Best would be outside-right against West Bromwich. Quite nerveless, he had a fair game.

He did not play for the first team again until Christmas, when he was summoned from Belfast by telegram back to Old Trafford for the return game on Boxing Day against Burnley, which United won 5—1, Best scoring his first goal. From now on he was never out of the team except because of injury . . . or discipline. The torrent of superlatives poured on him by the national press and everyone with whom he came in contact inevitably turned his head. As the party dates mounted, his form declined, and in September the following year, 1964, he was on the carpet in Busby's office, treatment reserved for special offences; those who are merely being dropped are taken on one side on a Monday or Tuesday after training into the dreaded referee's room next to the dressing room. This was different.

Busby quietly told him that he would have to tone down his night life and raise his application; for a while he was left out of the team in the hope that he would return wiser and improved. But though he was to become in less than two seasons one of the most illustrious names in Europe, the roundabout continued to gather speed with his fame—more parties, more girls, fast cars, a late-night crash 48 hours before a game and a prosecution, until finally he was back on that carpet. Busby, confronted with the greatest talent he had ever had in his club, told him point blank: 'You are lowering the name of Manchester United. Mend your ways, be professional—or I'll get rid of you.' And he meant it.

The slightly sentimental mask hid a realistic core. At the start of the 1963–4 season, immediately following defeat in the Charity Shield by Everton, Busby dropped Giles, Herd and Quixall: in came three youngsters, Moir, Chisnall and McMillan. Once again talent was expendable at Old Trafford, and Busby did not hesitate to exploit the fact. Out soon also went Setters, to be replaced by Stiles. Following the semi-final against Spurs in 1962, Stiles had made 31 League appearances the next season, only to be kept out of the Cup Final by injury.

Stiles was first spotted by Jimmy Murphy in a schoolboys' trial at Mansfield in 1956. 'There was this skinny little boy who seemed drawn to the ball as though by a magnet,' recalled Murphy. When he arrived at Old Trafford they said he did not so much tackle people as collide with them, until Busby discovered that his eyesight had been impaired in an accident and advised him to wear contact lenses. In spite of a rugged reputation which gained world-wide headlines, Stiles often fouled opponents partly because his timing was bad. But of this more later; Nobby Stiles was now an accepted cog in the improving United machine.

In the Cup-Winners Cup United made comfortable progress at first, beating Willem II from Holland 7—2 on aggregate. They then were drawn against Spurs, the holders, who though without Blanch-flower won the first leg 2—0 with goals by Mackay and Dyson. But in the second leg at Old Trafford the luckless Mackay broke his leg and United won 4—1, Herd and Charlton getting two each. At home to Sporting of Lisbon in the quarter-final, United built a 4—1 lead, with three goals from Law, including two penalties, and one from Charlton. On their first return to Europe they were as good as in the semi-final, and once again running for the Treble, including League and F.A. Cup. Before they went to Lisbon they had first to deal with West Ham in the F.A. Cup semi-final.

On the way to the F.A. semi-final they had had a comfortable run as far as the sixth round, defeating Southampton, Bristol Rovers and Barnsley, but were taken to three tough games by Sunderland before winning 5—1 at Huddersfield. The semi-final at Hillsborough was interesting for the fact that there was the prospect of two 17-year-olds being on the opposite sides at Wembley—Best, and Howard Kendall of Preston, who were playing Chelsea at Villa Park, both of them born on May 22, 1946. Preston beat Chelsea, but United went down 3—1 to West Ham in appalling conditions, the game being memorable for the decisive third goal by West Ham, when Moore came down the left touchline past two defenders to curl the ball to the waiting Hurst.

Undismayed, United set off for Lisbon, and the most disastrous performance in the club's European history. Within two minutes Dunne, a shade unluckily, handled, and Silva scored from the penalty. After 12 minutes there was a second goal, and United crumbled like melba toast. By the finish Sporting had put the necessary five goals past a derelict defence. It was a shattering experience. For a quarter of an hour back in the dressing room not a player took his shirt off or moved to the bath. They were stunned. For the first time ever, in Foulkes' recollection, Busby 'gave us a roasting immediately after a game'. Somebody said to Crerand: 'Never mind, there's always another time,' and received the sharp answer: 'There isn't. If I go on like this I'll wake up and find I'm 35, out of the game and never done anything.'

After the game, Busby left the team to themselves. Someone in Lisbon at the time who knew him well said: 'I think to some extent he blamed himself for trusting their ability too much and not laying down some plan.' Publicly, Busby excused the players as much as he could by saying: 'The boys left so much of themselves at home. The three matches against Sunderland took a lot out of them, and their semi-final at Hillsborough against West Ham on that terrible mud finally drained them mentally and physically. They were more affected by those games than we thought. The are sick with the shock of their defeat. I certainly do not blame individuals. We failed as a team, and I am sure the heavy programme of matches pulled us down.'

This was stretching generosity. Some of the players knew they had unnecessarily squandered a soft passage to the semi-finals. Law, it is said, went to bed without a word. United returned to London to beat Spurs, but in five days a season's ambitions had collapsed. In the League Liverpool, Manchester United, Everton, Spurs, Blackburn, Sheffield United, Nottingham Forest and Leeds had all led at one stage or another. United finished four points behind Liverpool in second place, good enough to gain a Fairs Cup place the following season.

In April Busby went into the transfer market once more, slightly impatient of his up-and-coming youngsters being ready, and bought John Connelly, a winger from Burnley, for £50,000. With Best on the other flank, this enabled Busby to make perhaps the most important of all the tactical switches in his 25 years as manager. Following Munich, he had moved Bobby Charlton from inside-forward to outside-left, in which position he had regained a regular England place, being voted the outstanding left-winger in the 1962 World Cup finals in Chile. The world's press gave him euphoric notices, and it was rumoured that Boca Juniors of Buenos Aires were anxious to sign him—with about as much chance as Tokyo Rovers of signing Busby.

Alf Ramsey, when he became England manager in 1963, continued to use Charlton as a winger, as had Walter Winterbottom, and Charlton played in nine of England's 11 matches in the 1963–4 season at outside-left. However, marriage and children had matured him; Busby sensed that he would ideally convert to an unfettered mid-field role, given the cover of the now almost statutory defensive wing-half—in this case the inimitable, demonic Nobby Stiles. Busby explained: 'There are few players in the world with Bobby's skill in being able to bring the ball under immediate control. There are few who can strike it with such accuracy. It was because of these two qualities, and the way he can come through from behind to use his shooting powers that he was switched to a mid-field role, where his game is now very reminiscent of Di Stefano.'

Ramsey used Charlton at inside-left in the first game of the 1964–5 season, when England beat Ireland 4—3 in Belfast, then switched him back to the wing against Holland and Scotland. It was against Scotland, at Wembley, that Bobby's brother Jack, the Leeds centre-half, and Stiles first appeared. With Wilson (Everton) and Byrne (West Ham) injured in the second half, Bobby dropped back to give an unexpectedly assured performance as a defender. He did not play again for England until the start of the 1965–6 season, but was then permanently included in his new deep-lying position, though often wearing the No. 9 or No. 11 shirt. His exhilarating runs from mid-field, together with shooting that put the clock back seven years, were features without which England would probably have never won the World Cup.

But, in the summer of 1964, Busby could now be confident that he was at last again beginning to get the reserve depth which was so fundamental to successful competition in Europe. Brennan, another convert from wing to half-back and then full-back, was competing with Dunne and Cantwell. In goal there were Gaskell, Gregg and Pat

Dunne (no relation but also from Dublin). Sadler, an amateur from Maidstone, was developing nicely as someone who could play anywhere from centre-forward to centre-half; coming up behind Connelly there were two young wingers, Anderson and Aston (son of the United coach and former full-back); and two full-backs, Noble and Burns, plus an inside-forward, Kinsey.

Law was now at the very peak of his powers, holding the Old Trafford crowds in the palm of his hand with the dramatic bravura of a matador. With Charlton and Crerand finding an instinctive understanding, not to mention the unpredictable wizardry of the youthful Best, Manchester United were once more the greatest draw in the land. By mid-season they were again heading for a treble—League, Cup and Fairs Cup. There was also a less happy side to their character developing.

Law, Stiles and Crerand and one or two others were letting the combination of tension and provocation get the better of them. Law, more often sinned against than sinning, was undoubtedly arrogant on the pitch—in strange contrast to his reticence off it—and with crowds always quick to respond to violent conduct by players, United's contribution to the game was not always virtuous. Things came to a head in the F.A. Cup semi-final against Leeds at Hillsborough.

Already, in November, Law had been suspended for a month for the second year running for abusive language to a referee during a game against Blackpool; wherever United played there seemed to be an undercurrent of anxious uncertainty about which way their mood would turn. In the early rounds of the Cup they beat Chester, Stoke and Burnley before meeting Wolves in the sixth round. This game saw them at their best. Wolves were two up in a quarter of an hour through McIlmoyle, but Law, though badly shaken in a first-half collision, made two goals and scored two with incomparable verve to give United a 5—3 victory.

The semi-final with Leeds was an almost continuous brawl. The referee, Dick Windle of Chesterfield, was too lenient, taking only two names when several players should have been sent off. United conceded 23 free-kicks to nine by Leeds. In the replay at Nottingham Windle was almost too strict. United gave away another 18 free-kicks, from the last of which, 90 seconds from the finish, Giles flighted the ball for Bremner to head the only goal of either game. This put Leeds in the final against Liverpool and inflicted United's third semi-final defeat in four years.

Public condemnation of the affair by Busby or Don Revie, Leeds' manager, a lead for which many people looked, was conspicuous by its absence. After the first match Roy Peskett of the *Daily Mail* wrote: 'In a life of football interest stretching back to 1927, I cannot remember seeing a match of such importance as an F.A. Cup semi-final so sordid.' After the second, Peskett's colleague Brian James commented: 'As United proved last night, they can still produce, at moments of crisis, football of the highest order.' Such were the club's two faces.

Meanwhile, things were humming in the League, in which it had been obvious since Christmas that the title lay between Leeds, Manchester United and Chelsea. Following the now notorious episode at Blackpool, when Chelsea's manager Tommy Docherty sent half the team home for climbing out of their hotel at night down a fire-escape, Chelsea, not surprisingly, slumped; with four matches to go, United were five points behind Leeds with a game in hand. United had struck a dizzy spell at the right moment, with six consecutive victories—Blackburn (0—5), Leicester (1—0), Leeds (0—1), Birmingham (2—4), Liverpool (3—0), Arsenal (3—1)—while Leeds faltered by losing to Sheffield Wednesday and drawing with Birmingham.

The first vital game was when United went to Leeds; Busby with his appetite for a gamble undiminished by the experience of Lisbon, told his team to 'make it all or nothing'. On a hard pitch swept by a strong wind, Connelly scored the only goal after a quarter of an hour. While Leeds were playing their final match at Birmingham, and drawing 3—3, United defeated Arsenal to ensure the title. Law tricked Ure to give Best the first goal and scored the other two himself. United could afford to lose their last match to Aston Villa—and did.

For only the fourth time since the League began in 1888, goal average decided the title, United being convincingly superior, with 2.28 to Leeds' 1.59; thereby also crushing the idea that they were not a good defensive side. Their record of 39 goals against was the best since Portsmouth's 38 when winning in 1950, while they scored 89, most of them spread with significant equality across the whole line: Connelly 15, Charlton 10, Herd 20, Law 28, Best 10. All eleven players were internationals. They were (3–3–4):

Dunne P. (Eire)

Dunne T. (Eire)   Foulkes (England)   Brennan (Eire)

Crerand (Scotland)   Charlton (England)   Stiles (England)

Connelly	Herd	Law	Best
(England)	(Scotland)	(Scotland)	(N. Ireland)

Thus seven years after Munich, United were once more League Champions and back in the European Cup, Busby's burning objective. Leeds, losing to Liverpool in the Cup Final, missed both domestic prizes. If Busby's countenance was always calm, the strain was there underneath. Bill Shankly, Liverpool's manager, recalled sitting next to him while Liverpool ambled to defeat at Old Trafford, conserving themselves for the Cup Final. As half-time approached Busby seemed agitated. 'What are you worried about,' chided Shankly, 'my boys haven't broken sweat. They'll be wearing overcoats in the second half.' With all his experience, Busby was still very much on edge even in what was a straightforward game.

There remained the Fairs Cup. United had beaten Djurgaardens of Sweden, Borussia Dortmund, Everton and Strasbourg and were now to meet Ferencvaros in the semi-final. The English season was already over: the players, inevitably were weary. In the first leg at Old Trafford United won 3—2 with goals by Law and Herd (2), lost the return 1—0, Crerand and Oroz being sent off; they also lost the toss for the venue for the play-off, and with the next season almost in sight had to return to Budapest. The only goal in the second game had been a penalty against Stiles, awarded when the ball struck him on the shoulder at such speed that he could not have got his hand to it had he wished. Then in the play-off, after an appalling journey by road from Vienna, Law missed an easy chance early on, Herd another when the score was 2—1 to Ferencvaros, which was how it stayed. In the final the Hungarians beat Juventus on their own ground in Turin.

In October the next season, when United were in London to play Spurs, the players surprised Busby with a small presentation in the hotel to mark his 20 years as manager—a cut-glass vase. Busby was so touched he had to go out into the corridor to compose himself before making a small speech of thanks. The players did not do so well by him on the field at White Hart Lane, losing 1—5. Would they be good enough to gain him his ambition in the European Cup?

In the first two rounds they had an easy passage, eliminating Helsinki and Vorwaerts of East Germany 9—2 and 5—1 on aggregate respectively. They were then drawn with Benfica, twice winners and twice beaten finalists in the past five years. It appeared formidable, the more so when Benfica led 1—0 in the first leg at Old Trafford with a goal from Augusto, straight from Eusebio's corner kick, after only a few minutes.

Herd had previously headed against a post from Best's free-kick, and it was Best who now put him through for the equaliser. An inspired moment by Charlton gave Law a second, and Foulkes, coming up to head home Cantwell's free-kick on the hour, made it 3—1. Always, however, there was the threat of Eusebio. Three times he nearly beat Gregg—back in the side with Cantwell—and finally created the chance for Torres to score from close in. Before the finish, Law, with successive headers, hit the bar and post, and United were left with only a 3—2 lead for the return.

In 18 home ties since 1960 Benfica had won every time, scoring 78 goals and conceding 13. They had only twice failed to score more than three, and only once conceded more than one. It was a daunting prospect that United faced.

Yet within a quarter of an hour they were sensationally three up, as errors by Benfica were punished with instant precision. After only six minutes Charlton was brought down by Germano, Benfica's centre-half, and from Dunne's free-kick Best headed a perfect goal. After 12 minutes Gregg cleared down the middle, Herd headed on, and Best ran through three men to score a superb second. Three minutes later an uninterrupted ripple of passes between Charlton,

Law and Connelly left Connelly with an open goal a few yards out.

Benfica had been destroyed. True, they were temporarily encouraged when Brennan misjudged a lob back to Gregg; but in the second half Crerand, put through by Law, and Charlton, beating three men, added further goals for a victory that dazzled the whole of Europe.

The following morning *Diario de Noticias* of Lisbon reported: 'Manchester United were fabulous in all that is most artistic, athletic, imaginative and pure in football.' Busby, more pleased that he would admit, re-stated his principle: 'I have always believed that a great team is built on blending the skills of great players. I have never been convinced that tactical systems and playing by numbers is a guarantee of success, and certainly not entertainment. The way they won gave me one of the greatest football moments of my life.'

This is not to say that United were without a system. Beforehand, Busby had told his players, remembering what had happened against Sporting, to 'hold them for the first twenty minutes, and then come at them from behind'. At half-time he told them to continue to go for goals, and not turn defensive; though it was obvious, as he said afterwards, that Best 'had cotton wool in his ears when we talked before the game. I was cross with him . . . almost. In the first quarter of an hour he had beaten them on his own. It was fantastic.'

The teams in Lisbon were (3–3–4):

BENFICA

Pereira

Cavem   Germano   Cruz

Silva   Coluna   Pinto

Eusebio   Torres   Augusto   Simoes

Best   Law   Herd   Connelly

Crerand   Charlton   Stiles

Brennan   Foulkes   Dunne

Gregg

UNITED

Unhappily, fate now took a hand. Before the semi-final against Partizan of Belgrade, Best injured his knee ligaments, and there was doubt about his fitness for the first away leg. Partizan, with seven internationals, were a far better side than most Western Europeans realised. Trailing 4—1 to Sparta of Prague in the quarter-final, they had won the second leg 5—0; they could not be taken lightly.

Before the game in Belgrade, Busby stated: 'We have never played for a draw before, and we will not start now. We shall be playing for a result.' In the event, discretion would have been the better part of valour. Unwisely in retrospect but true to his nature, Busby left the final decision on Best's fitness to the player himself, after tests in training had seemed to produce no ill-effect. Best, with the impetuosity of youth, was anxious to play; after five minutes he missed an easy chance, then made one for Law, who hit the bar from five yards. But Best had felt the stab of pain return to his knee, and was soon a limping passenger. Goals by Hasanagic and Becejac gave Partizan a useful lead: United returned home with uneasy minds, Best with a torn cartilage which required an operation and kept him out for the rest of the season.

Busby admitted as they departed: 'We played badly. I know it, the players know it, and we are very lucky to have a second chance next week. They were a far better side than we bargained for. Had we taken our chances in the first half, I don't think we would have been in this position. George's breakdown was unfortunate; all the evidence in training pointed to his being fit. It happened at the worst possible time, just after their first goal.'

There was an unexpected sequel to this. Best's father was a believer in faith healing, and Busby had to use all his persuasion to get George to a surgeon instead of a seance.

In the return leg Anderson replaced Best. Partizan now bolted all doors, and United's instinct failed where system, allied to their individual brilliance, might have succeeded. The only goal came 15 minutes from the end, a centre by Stiles being helped into the net by a defender: once more United had failed at the last stride. Fourth in the League behind Liverpool, Leeds and Burnley, it would be two seasons before they could have another tilt at that elusive European crown: two years in which their present brilliance might wane. For Busby it must have seemed his last and best chance had gone.

—11—

TRIUMPH AT LAST

Towards the end of June 1966, while England were on tour in Scandinavia making their final preparations for the World Cup, Denis Law went off to Ireland to play some golf. Before he left he casually dropped a time-bomb on Matt Busby's desk, to await his return from holiday in Portugal—a demand for a transfer.

Law's contract was due to end in August, both he and the club having the option of a further two years. Loyalty in football has always tended to go unrewarded, the more so since players became free to negotiate their own contracts—following a High Court case in 1961 between George Eastham and Newcastle United—and stood to make a profit by flitting from club to club.

Law knew, and Manchester United knew, that he had no peer in Britain. Why, therefore, should he not force United to give him, in a re-signing-on fee, what he could get by moving elsewhere, under pressure of the demand for a transfer? This might seem cynical, but footballers have a limited life—as Law was all too soon to discover—and if you cannot defeat the system you might as well exploit it. Law had reckoned without Busby.

The letter must have been opened, because Busby interrupted his holiday to return to Manchester. Finding that Law was pointing a gun at him, Busby, to his great credit, promptly fired the first shot by announcing: 'Law has said that unless he receives certain terms he wants a transfer. We are certainly not prepared to consider these, and are willing to receive offers for him.' Law might be big, but Manchester United were bigger. He now found himself confronted not merely with what he had not expected but what he most certainly did not want—the prospect of leaving Old Trafford.

For out there on the pitch, right arm raised aloft in triumphant salute and acknowledgement after one of those electrifying goals of his, Denis was King. Nowhere else could he expect the same acclaim, or have the benefit of such gifted colleagues as Best, Charlton and Crerand; nowhere else could he get the same basic wages of almost show-biz proportions. His bluff called, Law was suddenly defenceless. Put in the witness box, so to speak, he had no case.

Indeed, far from wanting to leave Old Trafford, he was more than anxious to stay, and spent a worrying few days before he was able to see Busby and come to mutually acceptable terms for a renewed contract, with an increased basic salary—a benefit which Busby proceeded to give, in proportion, to all the first-team squad. Having swiftly brought Law to heel, Busby was quick to forgive him. There were no public recriminations, and at the press conference to announce that Law would be remaining at Old Trafford, Busby said that he had gladly accepted an apology. Where Law could easily have been belittled, Busby allowed him the dignity of a gracious reunion. Law's response was to become the club's leading scorer for the fourth time in the five seasons since he joined them.

This stand on principle was to rebound on Busby in an unexpected way. In order to remain consistent he could not pay the substantial signing-on fees which might have secured him one or two players who became available the next season. He needed a centre-half, for instance, but when Mike England, of Wales and Blackburn, obtained his club's release, Busby was unable to sign him without risk of compromising himself with the rest of his players. The rule prohibiting signing-on fees, and giving players instead a share of transfer fees was not introduced till 1967.

However, in September he paid £60,000 for Alex Stepney from Chelsea, a goal-keeper who had started with the amateur club Tooting and Mitcham in London, and from there had gone to Millwall and Chelsea, for whom he played only one game. His job was to succeed the ageing Gregg, both Gaskell and Pat Dunne having fallen short of the standard needed at the top; at the end of the season, Busby was to admit: 'I don't think we would have won the Championship without him.'

England's victory in the World Cup, beating West Germany in the final 4—2 in extra time, had given football a surge of fresh popularity. The leap in attendances at Manchester United's matches was startling. By Christmas a million people had watched them home and away; the million mark for matches at Old Trafford was passed on April 18 against Southampton. The average home gate for '66-7 was 53,800, a post-war club record and over 15,000 up on the previous season, when they had been reigning League Champions.

Chelsea were the early pace-makers in the League, but United drew level at the end of November. On December 10 there was an event which drew little attention outside Manchester, but was yet another illustration of the constant stream of young players coming through from the junior ranks. When United drew 2—2 that afternoon with Liverpool only three players had cost large fees—Stepney, Crerand and Herd—while when Anderson came on as substitute there were six United players on the pitch who were under 20, all having risen from the side which won the Youth Cup in 1964. The team was: Stepney; Brennan, Noble; Crerand, Sadler, Dunne; Best, Charlton, Ryan, Herd, Aston. Connelly had by now moved to Blackburn.

United's last League defeat of the season was on Boxing Day, when they lost 1—2 at Bramall Lane to Sheffield United. From January 14, when they beat Spurs 1—0 at Old Trafford, they had a run of eight wins at home and eight draws away, the perfect formula for success. Critical matches were the 0—0 draw away to Liverpool, and a last-minute win at home to Nottingham Forest, their closest challengers; the vital goal came from . . . Law. It was an unlucky season for Forest, who finished second in the League and were beaten in the semi-final of the Cup by Spurs, who defeated Chelsea in the final.

On March 18 Herd broke his leg in the act of scoring his 16th goal of the season, against Leicester; Sadler, having played at centre-half with sufficient distinction to be in line for two England caps in the autumn, now moved into the forward line with equal effectiveness. The deciding match was against West Ham at Upton Park on

May 6. Within 25 minutes Law had scored twice, and United won in style 6—1. The team during the season in which Busby won his fifth Championship in 15 years was (3–3–4):

Stepney

Dunne   Foulkes (or Sadler)   Noble (or Brennan)

Crerand   Charlton   Stiles

Best   Law   Herd (or Sadler)   Aston

In the Cup they had lost in the fourth round 2—1 at home to Norwich, but apart from this lapse and an earlier 4—1 home defeat by Nottingham Forest, United had begun to develop a more conscious defensive technique, especially away from home, so clearly evident in the goal-less draw against Liverpool. Busby said: 'Talk that we always play it "off the cuff" is a fallacy. For the first 15 minutes we play to a calculated defensive system until we have gauged the strength of the opposition.' Yet regular observers of United would say this was no more than a concession to the contemporary demands for caution.

Away from home Busby would occasionally use Sadler in a forward's shirt as an extra mid-field player. In addition to the continued improvisation that delighted the crowds there were signs of modifications in Busby's tactical outlook, yet forced on him, reluctantly. There were already signs, before his most famous triumph, that age was overtaking him. Attention to minor detail off the field, however, remained unaltered. When Eric Taylor, Sheffield Wednesday's general manager, injured in a road accident, was in hospital at the time of United's Championship celebration banquet, he received by first post the following morning a menu signed by Busby and the United directors, wishing him a swift recovery.

United now departed on a tour of America, Australia and New Zealand. They took with them all the outstanding young players on the fringe of the first team—Kidd, Burns, Fitzpatrick, Gowling, Edwards, Rimmer. It gave them invaluable experience, which was to prove a sound move sooner than Busby would have wished. Kidd, a tall, powerful inside-forward of 18, was a particular success. Coming from the same school as Stiles, Collyhurst in Manchester, he scored 10 goals, was then picked for the Charity Shield against Spurs at the start of the season, and kept his place.

The tour renewed Busby's faith in the scope for producing his own players often enough and of the necessary standard. As he said: 'If they are good enough, they are old enough, and I have no fears about taking a chance. But I do try to slip them in when the team is doing reasonably well, and I take the precaution of arranging some cover around them if they need a helping hand.'

During this tour there was a real indication of weariness creeping up on Busby. Always one to honour all public engagements, he disappeared one morning, leaving the party, and spent the whole day alone in a boat on a lake, as though he were taking time off to recharge batteries.

Now back in the European Cup, Busby was anxious to strengthen the side, in spite of the wealth of material available from the junior ranks. During the season he made attempts to buy five forwards, including, it was reported, Johnstone, right-winger of Celtic, who had just become the first British club to win the European Cup, and Hurst, the West Ham and England centre-forward who had scored a hat-trick in the World Cup final. None of the enquiries was successful, and so the younger players came more and more into the picture as United forged their way towards the double of League and European Cup. Their F.A. Cup hopes ended abruptly when they were beaten—without the injured Foulkes—in the third round by Spurs, who dropped the renowned but fading Greaves at Old Trafford and brought him back for the replay at White Hart Lane, winning 1—0.

At one stage during the season United had opened a five-point lead in the League, but from the middle of February to April they suffered a run of five defeats in eight games, so that Manchester City, carefully nurtured back towards respectability by Joe Mercer and Malcolm Allison, had drawn level with two matches to go. In their penultimate games City won 3—1 away to Spurs, United 6—0 at home to Newcastle. It now seemed that the odds were much in United's favour: while their remaining fixture was at home to lowly Sunderland, City were away to Newcastle. City finished like true champions, with a 4—3 win at St. James Park, while United were beaten 2—1 by Sunderland. Yet their attendances were an all-time League record average of 57,549, beating Newcastle's previous figures.

The season had had its complications. Law, sent off in October with Ure of Arsenal, received his third heavy suspension, this time six weeks. Then came an injury to Stiles, and a knee operation which kept him out of action for over two months. Kidd had already stepped with astonishing maturity into Herd's shoes. Now, with Brennan's form at full-back in doubt, two more of the youth squad made the transition to the first team with barely a ripple on the surface of its performance.

Francis Burns, a Scottish full-back, adapted himself equally well there or in mid-field, where Stiles' vacancy was largely occupied by John Fitzpatrick, another Scot. Yet while the side was steady enough in the weekly League programme, the lack of big-match experience among the youngsters inevitably resulted in a desperation creeping into their game at times; Fitzpatrick fell into the over-exuberant ways of Stiles.

The European Cup passage had been smooth enough at first, with Hibernian of Malta beaten 4—0 at Old Trafford—two each from Charlton and Sadler—and then allowed the honour of holding the English masters to a goal-less draw at home, where a poor pitch was no incentive for United to give an exhibition in anything but gentle self-preservation. The next round against Sarajevo was altogether different, with United glad to return from Yugoslavia with a goalless draw in which the rules were barely observed by either side. After 25 minutes Musemic of Sarajevo seemed to have forced a shot over the line before Stepney recovered the ball, but a goal was refused by the referee. For the return, Fitzpatrick was under suspension for domestic League offences, so Burns played in mid-field with Brennan at full-back. Aston scored when Sarajevo's 'keeper failed to hold a header by Best, who was soon involved in an affray with Mustic. Best, I thought, was guilty but undetected, and when Prljaca tried to balance the books with a Machiavellian foul on Best he was duly sent off. Best scored a second, when the ball seemed obviously first to have gone out of play, but Sarajevo, though a man short, fought back and were rewarded with a goal by Delalic. United were through, but devoid of distinction.

Clearly the team had problems, not least a lack of assurance—more bluntly, *class*—in defensive positions, and Busby must have felt that for the fourth time the vision of the European trophy was merely mocking him. While Stiles was now back in action, Law was troubled by a knee injury which kept him out of the quarter-final against Gornik of Poland, who had eliminated Kiev, themselves the conquerers of Celtic, the holders.

Coming straight to Old Trafford from the mid-winter break in their season, Gornik were less fit and would have been beaten out of sight but for their keeper Kostka, who saved everything that Charlton, Best, Kidd and Aston fired at him. United forced 20 corners without success and would have had a goal down had not Lubanski, Gornik's mercurial inside-forward, shot feebly when perfectly placed. Stepney held the ball almost with a yawn.

It was not until an hour had run that Best finally put United in front, beating two men in a way which showed he would have been even more a sensation had he played 10 years before, when defences were rather more ingenuous. And that was all, until, in the last minute, Crerand lobbed into the goal-mouth, the ball was headed out, Ryan mis-hit a shot and from a seemingly harmless position Kidd sent the ball slowly through a maze of legs and over the line. But for this soft goal which doubled their lead, United would have had little hope when they travelled to snow-bound Poland a fortnight later.

Before leaving for the return leg, Busby, knowing that without a fit Law the chances of winning the Cup were slim, made a secret bid for Geoff Hurst, the West Ham and England striker who had scored a hat-trick in the World Cup final against West Germany. Hurst, with his immense courage and power, was the personification of the new-era centre-forward—a man who could take a continual pounding from the defenders but still had the skill to snap up chances in tight situations. The day United left for Poland, Busby phoned West Ham. Ron Greenwood, the manager, was out, so Busby left the following message with the secretary: '£200,000 for Geoff Hurst: yes or no? Please telephone or telegram your answer to Katowice. Busby.'

When Greenwood discovered the message it came as a bombshell.

For years he had patiently built a team at West Ham which was second to none in England in its concept of football as a game of skill. It failed regularly to win trophies because Greenwood refused to compromise with his conviction that more physical aggression had little place in the game. To lose Hurst would be to lose what chance there was for repeating the club's achievement of winning the F.A. Cup in 1964 and the European Cup-Winners Cup the following year. His answer, cabled immediately to Busby, was short and to the point: 'No. Greenwood.' He resented Busby's impersonal approach, but nothing would have made him reply differently. Manchester United would have to hope for Law's recovery.

After one look at the pitch at Chorzow, near Katowice, Busby tried unsuccessfully to find the Italian referee, Lo Bello, to attempt to have the game postponed. Given no alternative by the conditions, by modest lead, and a team which leaned too heavily on the fantasies of Best, Busby decided, for the first time in 28 European Cupties, that this would have to be a rearguard action. It was not that he was swallowing his principles; he was ruled by circumstance. In the event United, with Stiles and Fitzpatrick in their element as spoilers, survived but narrowly. Half-way through the second half Stepney was penalised for doing what the changed goal-keeping law quite clearly allows—putting the ball down and dribbling it forward towards the edge of the area—and after United had failed to clear the indirect free kick, Lubanski scored via the cross-bar. For the fourth time in four attempts United were in the semi-finals.

Busby's comment afterwards was more an exercise in public relations than an accurate reflection of what had happened. 'A marvellous performance, one of our greatest nights,' he said. 'We came here to do a job, to contain them, and we did it well, although the conditions were all against us.' If the team had scrambled through a little luckily it was that much more important for them to believe it had been marvellous; realistic appraisal could come later, though the dream of not just winning the European Cup but doing so 'gloriously' was barely tenable at this point.

The draw for the semi-finals ensured that United must prove themselves worthy if they were to win, for they were paired, as the first time in 1957, with Real Madrid, no longer a power but at least the winners two seasons before in 1966, against Partizan. United were given the added disadvantage of playing the first leg at home, at the end of which they led by a single goal from Best. Busby said, 'I think we will win because I am convinced we are the better side.' Some felt he was too easily convinced, considering that at Old Trafford Real had been without their best forward, Amancio, under suspension, and that he would return for the second leg.

In the first leg Law was but a shadow; the reflexes slowed, the snap near goal no longer a thing of wonder and fury. A suspect knee was again troubling him, and he was omitted from the game in Madrid, where Foulkes, having recovered from his own knee injury, returned at the age of 36 for his 29th of United's 32 European ties. Sadler kept his place, as an extra defender instead of Law; Brennan came in at full-back in place of Burns, who had played in the first seven ties.

Between the two ties I had flown with Busby and several other journalists to Lisbon to see the semi-final first leg between Benfica and Juventus, from which it was clear that Benfica, though winning 2—0, had slipped even farther than we had heard. As Busby said: 'They can still turn on the magic occasionally, but I don't think they are as good as when we beat them two years ago. They looked slow in mid-field in the first half. Obviously the big one for us is next week. If only we can survive that I feel we have a good chance at Wembley.' What he did not say, of course, was that neither were United as good.

For the second time running in an away leg, Busby conceded that defensive tactics would be prudent, in spite of the fact that United led by only a single goal. The performance in Chorzow had helped persuade him that if United could win going backwards, so to speak, then however much he might dislike the system, it was in his club's interest. So in Madrid the only two players lying up the field were Kidd and Best. For half an hour the plan worked well.

Then, from a free-kick by Amancio, Pirri headed past Stepney; an error by Brennan allowed Gento to make it 2—0; and though Zoco sliced Dunne's centre past his own 'keeper, Amancio quickly scored again, fooling two defenders, to give Real a 3—1 lead at half-time. As United had lost to Sunderland the previous Saturday, and with that defeat the League title, their only way to remain in the European Cup the next season was to win and qualify as holders. As the teams went in for the interval, nothing could have been more remote. It was now that Busby pulled a master stroke.

In the dressing room he told the players: 'We've been playing a defensive game, which we don't do very well. But we're only 3—2 down on aggregate, so let's go out and attack. Enjoy yourselves. You've done well to get so far, so don't worry.' The team could hardly believe their ears; with Real having achieved such demoralising command in the previous 15 minutes, to go out and attack invited disaster. As Best observed later: 'I don't think he's really ever heard of the word defend.'

So now Sadler switched to an attacking role, and it was he who scored to shake Real out of their complacency. Crerand lobbed the ball forward and a header by Foulkes fell in no-man's-land, between Real's keeper and the other defenders. Before either could move, Sadler had appeared with that stealthy stride to glance the ball home. Now the scores over the two games were level, with just under a quarter of an hour to go.

At a throw-in, Crerand stood stuttering on the line. Foulkes, abandoning all caution, went for the throw, and thus drew two men with him, which allowed Best more space with the ball than he had been given throughout the game. Let Foulkes pick up the story:

'Having taken these two fellows with me, I kept going as George went off down the line. It was a great run and he left both Sanchis and Zoco. I could hear them on the trainer's bench screaming at me to get back, but I kept on and when George reached the line I called for the ball. I didn't expect it to come, but he must have seen me, and put it right in my path.' So Bill Foulkes, a survivor with Charlton and Gento of that other semi-final between the two clubs 11 years before, now scored his only European Cup goal to give United the chance to win the trophy. It was, as they say, too good to be true. Louis Edwards, United's chairman, had been watching the game with George Sturrup. Now they made the long walk round the

Barnebeu Stadium to the dressing rooms, and Sturrup recalls: 'It was a moving sight. There were Bobby Charlton and Matt, in separate corners of the dressing room, both crying. I went up to Matt to congratulate him, and he just kept saying, "I can't help it, I can't help it." I shall always remember that evening.'

When he had had time to compose himself Busby said: 'This team proved it had heart in the way it came back, as only great teams can, to win what seemed a lost cause. I think that this heart can win the European Cup. To defend, as we did at the start, was the right thing, even if it looked as if the tactics had gone wrong. I would play it exactly the same way if we turned back the clock. You just cannot leave yourself wide open. We had to play it tight while we were in front.'

This, clearly, contradicts what Busby has previously held—that defence was not only bad tactics but poor entertainment. Even though he reversed his battle orders at half-time, what brought him to the point where he was prepared to compromise? In retrospect I feel it must be that, in his fourth semi-final, the instinct to win at all costs overruled the grand conception of football as a competitive, artistic entertainment. The football world, which for 23 years had admired his unfaltering loyalty to attack, could hardly complain if he now temporarily took refuge in defence. Besides, the attacking, gambling flourish reasserted itself. All his life Busby, quietly, had been a bit of a gambler. Someone once said of him: 'If there were two beetles crossing the carpet, he'd bet on them.' In the Rechts der Isar Hospital in Munich, where they nursed the life back into him, the surgeons recalled, smilingly, that 'he was always very interested in the horses'. Now, at half-time in a game of football in Madrid, his courage to take a calculated risk had brought him to the brink of his greatest ambition.

The final against Benfica was played at Wembley, an obvious advantage to Manchester United, but one which previous teams had had when playing in their own national stadium. At least Benfica had the experience of playing at Wembley before, when they lost the 1963 final to A.C. Milan. Busby, though he had a difficult decision, kept the same team as in Madrid, leaving out young Burns. Law was to have an operation on his knee, a loss to the side which most clubs would have looked upon as insuperable. Imagine Santos without Pélé, or Benfica themselves without Eusebio. The teams lined up that warm May evening as follows:

MANCHESTER UNITED (4–3–3)

Stepney

Brennan   Foulkes   Stiles   Dunne

Crerand   Charlton   Sadler

Best   Kidd   Aston

Simoes   Eusebio   Torres   Augusto

Coluna   Graca

Cruz   Jacinto   Humberto   Adolfo

Henrique

BENFICA (4–2–4)

Usually, before a night match, the United team went to bed for a sleep in the afternoon, Jack Crompton having to wake them with a shake in time for a light meal at 4.30. On the afternoon of the final they were all up again within half an hour or so, wandering about at their hotel in Berkshire, the tension intolerable. Kidd recalled: 'It wasn't just that this was the final. I think everyone had this feeling that we *had* to win to finish the job for The Boss, after all this time. You didn't have to talk about it, but however old you were, you knew just what it meant to him. I don't think it really entered our heads that we were playing for ourselves.'

Because Busby has always considered that anything done for him was done for the club, he would have been as proud of this spirit— which many years before he had set out to create—as of victory itself.

On the Wembley pitch where England had won the World Cup two years before, United now set out to keep the European Cup in Britain, urged by the unbroken roar of a 100,000 crowd. Never had Wembley heard such a noise as now, and Benfica soon knew the tide was running against them. In quick response to the pace of Aston and the wiles of Best they unsheathed the weapons of anxiety:

calculated late tackles sent United's wingers flying, Cruz crudely reminding one of the way he had successfully cut down Pélé in the World Cup. Suddenly this august scene was just like any Saturday cup-tie on a public pitch; fear of defeat reduced the rhythm of both sides, for Stiles permitted no formality in his treatment of Eusebio. Once, twice, three times Stiles stopped him like a pitchfork going into a turnip; the second time he was admonished by the referee, Lo Bello, when Eusebio blatantly feigned injury; the third time he was allowed to get away with the worst of the lot. Lo Bello refereed like a conductor wearing ear-plugs, and when half-time arrived without injury or temper it was a relief more than a surprise.

Both back lines had been vulnerable; United to the threat in the air from two-metres tall Torres and the phenomenal power of Eusebio when shooting from up to 30 yards, Benfica to the esoteric shafts of Best and the runs from deep positions by Charlton and Sadler. Eusebio had shuddered the crossbar, Sadler had put the ball wide when clean through with only Henrique to beat. A great occasion had so far produced only average football.

Ten minutes after half-time United went ahead as Dunne and Sadler worked the ball down the left and Sadler's cross was glanced by the airborne Charlton beyond the reach of Henrique, who had come out as if to intercept and had no chance to recover. It was rare for Charlton to head a goal, but he could not have picked a more important moment. If Benfica had fallen from their former pinnacle they still had the instinct for counter-attack, and now United were under the whip. Yet the result could have been put beyond doubt had a shot by Sadler, with Henrique beaten, not hit the 'keeper on the foot and spun over the bar.

Grateful for this escape, Benfica drew level 10 minutes from time when Torres headed down to Graca, and now it seemed that United might crumble. They would have done so had Eusebio not chosen to try to burst the net a few minutes from the finish with Stepney utterly at his mercy. Stepney had come out too far, was frantically trying to get back, when Eusebio hit the ball with all his ferocious power from the edge of the area. He could have placed it, but his wish to score a spectacular goal instead of a simple one gave Stepney the chance to make a brilliant save close to his left. In that split-second decision by Eusebio, Benfica lost their chance to win. Eusebio, his sportsmanship undiminished by the successful aggression of Stiles, ran to congratulate Stepney.

United held on till the end of normal time, then sank to the ground—to outward appearances exhausted and in no shape to endure the gruelling demands of extra time. There are two opposed views about what was really happening out there on the pitch. Stiles claimed that 'we were shattered and Benfica would have won if there'd been another ten minutes, but then we saw they were in even more of a bad way, just like the Germans in the World Cup.' Crerand, on the other hand, felt that United would now have the edge, and that taking a rest was merely sensible while Ted Dalton, Wilf McGuinness, Jack Crompton and others massaged their weary limbs. If United lacked the refinement and deadly finishing of former winners such as Real Madrid and Benfica themselves, they were now going to have to find reserves of courage and strength—a cliché perhaps, but found only in teams of character.

United were not, in the strict sense, a great footballing side. They had one player of pure, unrivalled brilliance in Best; another, past his prime but still a peerless artist, in Charlton; Crerand, an astute tactician; and eight others prepared to give all they possessed. Without Law, watching on television in hospital, United were not even as formidable as they had been two years before: that was when they *should* have won. Yet if in their eight previous ties that season they had never reached the heights, they did so now in extra time, scoring three times in 10 minutes for an exultant climax.

Busby, during the brief interval, was calmness itself, lessening the stress on his men rather than magnifying it. 'You're giving them the ball too often,' he said. 'You're being too hasty. Try to keep possession, play for width. Don't stand off, come and meet the ball, and keep attacking.' In the finishing straight he was not going to start looking over his shoulder.

The team responded instantly, as in Madrid. Within moments Stepney, receiving the ball from a back pass, cleared high down the middle, Kidd glanced the ball on, and Best, with a swerving run that stopped 100,000 hearts, glided past Cruz and round Henrique in an arc to send the ball scurrying into an empty net as Henrique in vain flung himself back towards his line. Now Aston, scorning all those who had so meanly derided him earlier in the season, swept past Adolfo yet again to force a corner; Charlton floated the ball across, Kidd's first header was palmed out by Henrique, but, twisting in the air like a salmon, Kidd put a second header beyond the 'keeper's reach. Seldom has any boy had such a momentous birthday as the 19-year-old Kidd. From Kidd's swift break, Charlton now glanced home the fourth goal, and United had, after all the uncertainty, won a memorable victory.

Charlton, overcome with relief, the tension of responsibility and years of heartache suddenly released, collapsed on the ground in emotion. Busby embraced each player in turn; they had not merely won the European Cup, but had given substance to a dream which a decade beforehand had seemed irreparably destroyed. As the tears of pride filled Busby's eyes his mind went back to those who had been so tragically denied their ultimate goal . . . Byrne, Edwards, Taylor, Colman, Whelan, Jones, Pegg, Bent. Their loss, which came in pursuit of this very prize, would not drift each year a little further into obscurity. It had been given new meaning: they were no longer the sad part of a story without an end. Some of the parents of those who had died were with United at the banquet that followed Wembley; they too could share the sense of fulfilment. With Matt Busby, they could be proud.

—12—
TARNISHED IMAGE

As the the new European Champions, the next hurdle for Manchester United was the World Club Championship, in which the European winners meet the South American Club Cup winners. This competition, played on a two-leg basis, began in 1960 and the early years saw some breathtaking matches of unsurpassed skill between Santos of Brazil or Penarol of Uruguay and Benfica or Real Madrid. Then slowly, as negative attitudes crept more and more into the game in keeping with the ever-mounting financial stakes, the World Club Championship became an annual battlefield, culminating in 1967 with three disgraceful games, including a play-off in Montevideo, between Celtic of Glasgow and Racing Club, Buenos Aires. There were many who considered that the moment had come to end a competition which did little but harm to the game.

Celtic were perhaps unlucky; feeling in Buenos Aires against British soccer was running high, following the elimination the previous year of Argentina by England in the World Cup quarter-finals, Rattin, the Argentinian captain, being sent off in controversial circumstances. Uruguay also felt that they had received a rough deal from European referees in the World Cup, so the mood throughout South America was ill-disposed towards Britain. Celtic, though far from innocent, caught some of this emotional back-lash. What were the prospects for Manchester United, now due to meet Estudiantes de la Plata in Buenos Aires?

Matt Busby, always eager for new experience for his players and keen to succeed where Celtic had failed, put one point of view when he said: 'I believe that one will only break these continental barriers by playing more, not less.' Amid general misgivings, United departed for the first leg against Estudiantes in September: the wisdom of the decision to play was soon in doubt. Yet before considering these two matches which brought United nothing but trouble—if you exclude a £60,000 gate at Old Trafford—it is worth analysing Busby's attitude towards discipline on the field over the years. He had been persistently accused of lenience towards his players, and these accusations were now growing.

Let us go back to the beginning of the Fifties. In the early years after the war there were, of course, dirty players, as there always will be. Everyone knew who they were, and kept out of their way if possible. The difference in those days was that if you were kicked you did not the next instant swing round and fell the opponent with a boot or even a fist in a fit of wild retaliation. Ron Greenwood always said: 'You could afford to be more patient then. I've waited three years in my day to get my own back on a fellow who had "done" me. I always tell my players, "It's better to have a long memory than a short temper."'

The pressures then were not so huge. There was a maximum wage for players, and directors and managers were not lusting for success. It was possible to finish 14th in the League and for the club's supporters still to think it had been a good season if the football had been entertaining. In two decades, the picture altered vastly. Not to qualify for one of the three European competitions was now failure: if you were not in the top six you were nothing. With every match for a major club played in an atmosphere of almost unbearable tension it was inevitable that tempers would deteriorate as injustice, whether by opponent or referee, became potentially more costly—either to the players on huge bonuses or the club striving for 'big-time' status.

When Bill Foulkes came into the Manchester United side in 1952 one of his first matches was against Cardiff City at Ninian Park. The Cardiff outside-left was a player called Edwards, fast and clever and with a reputation for making a monkey out of full-backs. Although United had set new standards with ball-playing full-backs, Carey and Aston—Spurs, too, with Alf Ramsey—full-backs were still apt to be that anachronism, the slowest men of the field marking the fastest. Foulkes decided to let Edwards know who was master, and at the first opportunity clobbered him with a tackle which shook every bone. At half-time he was severely rebuked by Busby: 'Never lose your head, and remember we try to play football.'

Busby, himself a cultured player, did not at this stage of his managerial career believe in physical aggression. Johnny Carey reflected: 'He firmly believed that the game should be played fairly by everyone. It amazes me that some of the players in the last few years have been allowed to get away with what they have. I feel he should have fined offenders more. This increase in rough play within the club may possibly have been the result of more players being bought from outside.' Foulkes echoed this when he said: 'Since the maximum wage was removed the performance has gone up, but the spirit has, I think, gone down.'

In many ways Busby was a contradiction, the tolerant perfectionist. On and off the field he was anxious that his players should be exemplary; it hurt him if they did not respect his authority. If he was very much The Boss, the compassionate side of his nature made it difficult for him to be really severe with misdeeds which he knew were no more than momentary excesses. Always conscious of the good name of the club, the problem was trying to keep discipline private, not to allow it to magnify that which it was supposed to cure.

Wilf McGuinness remembered the time when he and others, including Giles and Brennan, were involved in an escapade with some water pistols when they stopped their car several times to ask some girls the way, then soaked them and drove off—a harmless enough prank. The car and the players were recognised and in no time they were summoned to Busby's house. Busby was dressing them down when Jean interrupted . . . 'Now remember when you were young, Matt.' The subsequent discipline was paternal rather than proprietory. Another time, McGuinness had a passing interest in acquiring a share of a night-club business, and Busby, gently dissuading him, said: 'You know enough about night-clubs without owning one.' McGuinness was left wondering how he found out.

As George Best said, a little ruefully: 'It seems you can't do a thing in Manchester without his knowing.'

There were many times when for the sake of short-term effect Busby could have stamped on some of the players. There was an incident on tour in Italy in 1963 when a hotel door was broken during some horse-play late in the evening. Maurice Setters remembered Busby 'sprinting down the corridor after the culprits, but by the time he found those involved they were all in bed. No one would own up, and since he could not be certain who was guilty, he was not going to punish them at random. But had he known who it was they would have gone straight home.' Noel Cantwell, for several years the club captain, recalled: 'I've known him say, when club rules were broken, "I don't mind about the European Cup or anything else, but you've got to toe the line." Yet you could never find anyone more understanding.'

Several of the players, Charlton, Law and in particular Best, were the victims from time to time of vicious anonymous letters, addressed either to them or occasionally to the manager. Charlton was once called to see Busby and confronted with an anonymous phone call accusing him of being out in the early hours drinking double Scotches unlimited. 'True or false?' demanded Busby. 'I've never drunk Scotch in my life,' replied Charlton. 'Good,' said Busby, 'I gave the fellow a volley.'

Such things, of course, can usually be kept private, but what happens on the field is inevitably public. And on his players' misdeeds on the field Busby's attitude was increasingly equivocal over the years. Murphy said: 'I think he has become more tolerant since Munich. One of the difficulties is that anything which a Manchester United player does always gets more publicity than it would with most other clubs. This is something The Boss has to live with.'

It is possible to argue that Busby was both weak and strong—weak not be more strict with those who consistently broke the laws, strong not to yield too often to misinformed and misguided public comment. He believed, like any English manager, that physical contact was an essential part of the game: that you cannot play without the ball, and that to get it you have to win it in the tackle, even if he himself was no great tackler and had to rely more on interception. It is my opinion that Duncan Edwards, but for the Munich crash, would have been an increasingly controversial character in European soccer. All those who knew him best claim, and without any ulterior motive, that Duncan was not a dirty player. What they mean is that he was not *intentionally* a dirty player, for he was one of the greatest sportsmen. But whether he tackled within the laws as they are written—and more and more we have to ask whether the British are not incorrect in their interpretation of this—is open to doubt. Again and again, in reports of those matches in which the massive 'Big Dunc' indelibly left his mark on European soccer, English writers would report that 'after one of Edwards' tackles, *devastating but quite fair*, so-and-so hit the ground like a sack of potatoes'. We have Willy Meisl's testimony that Edwards was one of the most noble players of all times, but Europeans in general were not quite happy about those tackles, which, of course, were perfectly fair in Britain.

Since the late fifties it has not been possible for any team to achieve greatness without one or two hard men. Real Madrid's centre-half, Santamaria from Argentina, was as tough as they come; the great Spurs team relied heavily on the physical tenacity of Mackay and Smith to supplement the refinement of Blanchflower, White and Greaves. Busby quite clearly accepted this side of the game when appointing Jimmy Murphy as his assistant. If Busby gave the team their tactical ideals it was Murphy who gave them teeth.

I would be the first to agree that to some extent Manchester United have been victims of their own success. Criticism of their 'dirty' players has been fanned by envy of their success; and the principle of *noblesse oblige*, that the higher you stand the more you must set an example, is a difficult one to honour in football where you are only as good as your last result. In many instances the same acts by the same players would have received less publicity had they been playing for any other club, though this is not to excuse them. They should be punished by the same yardstick as any other, but at the same time they must not be considered *more* guilty. The problem was, of course, intensified by the huge crowds which supported Manchester United, and the streak of hooliganism which existed at

Old Trafford as elsewhere. But there is plenty of evidence that crowd violence is not derived from violence on the field, merely encouraged by it: this is a problem for society, not just football managers.

Over the years Busby realised that if he was to compete with other leading teams he had to have players who were competitors: if the players he possessed with outstanding skills such as Charlton, Viollet and Best were to stand a chance, there had to be others around who could provide the physical resilience. In Denis Law, signed from Torino in 1962, Busby suddenly had someone who fitted both categories—a man of astonishing skill and reflexes, yet with it immensely brave and aggressive. His arrival coincided with a steady increase in controversy surrounding United, and came to a head in the autumn of 1963.

Ever since Munich, United's reputation had been far from clean. In the remainder of the 1957–8 season, on the way to the F.A. Cup Final, the side hastily assembled by Murphy contained several players who seemed to have the idea that the tragedy had given them a licence to ignore the laws. By the time that Cantwell, Setters and Law had joined the club, and with Stiles now on the fringe of things, the team was gaining a name for itself which should have had Busby concerned if not worried. But in an interview with the *Daily Express* in September 1963, he came out strongly in defence of Cantwell, Setters and Law in a manner which suggested he condoned their more excessive actions. He said: 'If you took the right of challenge away from these players, you would be taking away much of what makes them internationals, and football would be the poorer for it.' Yet his opinion of them as footballers was such that within a short time Cantwell and Setters had been replaced in the team.

Hardly had Busby spoken than, in November, Law was suspended for 28 days for kicking an opponent, the first of three heavy suspensions he was to receive. He was suspended for 28 days again the following November, and for six weeks in 1967. I remember writing in defence of Law in 1964, saying that he was more sinned against than sinning; that it was the very nature of his lightning reactions that resulted in his being consistently fouled by defenders who were too slow to match him; and that his unrivalled competitive instinct consequently made him react equally swiftly to injustices. Sometimes, certainly, he did illegal, intentional things that deserved reprimand; but he was caught up, like other great players, in a system which allowed, with the help of permissive referees, too much freedom to the destroyers of the game at the expense of its truly creative artists. Busby went out of his way to thank me for the article; he has always been quick to feel persecuted by adverse criticism. One of Law's colleagues at this period considers that only Busby could have kept Law in the game; that such was the player's arrogant contempt for opposition and authority alike, when he was on the field, that he would soon have become an impossible liability. Certainly he went three years without suspension, but it was a near thing in 1965 in the F.A. Cup semi-final against Leeds.

Law was one of the principal figures in a game which ran along barely the right side of a brawl, and I wondered whether I had been right to defend him. Leeds were equally guilty, but here was the worst exhibition I had ever seen from Manchester United. The episode could have been given a little dignity had Busby, at an appropriate moment afterwards, shown his disapproval, but publicly, and I felt regrettably, he remained silent. Quite apart from the tarnished image of his club, there was growing concern at the effect their behaviour was having upon the crowds. J. L. Manning wrote in the *Daily Mail*: 'Police at Old Trafford might have a splendid detection toy with closed-circuit television cameras sweeping the terraces for offenders, but I would be happier if Mr. Busby kept a closer watch on his players. There are few clubs whose footballers have been more troublesome than his, and none which attracts such large crowds. This is an explosive mixture.'

Of course, crowd violence existed elsewhere, but one did not hear it said that Bill Shankly, Harry Catterick, Ron Greenwood and Bill Nicholson should be responsible for the behaviour of public citizens who watched the games of Liverpool, Everton, West Ham and Spurs. But this is the price of fame. If Busby was happy to accept the plaudits for the team's success, he had also to be blamed in part for their indiscretions, which were too many to be coincidence. In the 10-year period between Munich and the winning of the European

Cup more than 20 Manchester United players were sent off the field, and the teams collected between them nearly 70 cautions. It is ironic that while Matt Busby epitomised what we all mean when we talk about 'a good man', some of his players, on the field, had been very much the reverse.

If there was a reason for his not taking more positive action it was probably that, seeing his most brilliant players such as Charlton, Law, Best and others receive the most disgraceful treatment from opposing teams almost every week, often without legal protection from the referee, he had turned a Nelsonian eye on the offences of his own 'hard' men. Bobby Charlton was the greatest sportsman of a generation in his acceptance of every decision, or lack of it, and of unlimited abuse from crudely inferior opposition. Best, with a streak of Irish fire in him, was less inclined to tolerate this abuse, and to a lesser extent than Law this landed him in trouble. Next to Pélé, I know no player who had to endure more persistent provocation and physical intimidation than Best, yet such was his pride in his own ability, in his own incredible balance and ball control, that so long as it was possible he would stay on his feet. 'If I was prepared to "dive" like some other players I could probably get seven or eight penalties a season, but all I've had is two in two years,' he said. Often it should have been two in one match. The same abuse was later to be inflicted on Maradona.

When Law was sent off in 1967, together with Ure of Arsenal, he had been provoked from the start of the game. It was the opinion of experienced observers that firm action earlier in the game might have prevented the incident. That was one thing. But it was quite another, and in many people's view wrong, for Busby to seek Law's release from his subsequent suspension in order that he might take part in the European Cup-tie against Sarajevo. Whatever he might have felt about the merits of the case, it was Busby's obligation to accept the decision; if he disputed authority, what could he expect from his players and those who watched them?

The winning of the European Cup did not find a diminishing of United's reputation. If Stiles had now learned discretion in his tack-ling he was still given to violent gestures of disapproval when penalised by the referee, and for the foreign press he was still an *enfant terrible*, his appearance in any foreign capital a cause for hysterical warnings to the home team. When England played in Rome in the finals of the European Nations Cup in the summer of 1968 against Russia, Stiles was booed from the moment he appeared on the pitch by the Roman crowd who had never previously seen him. He of all people could hardly shout 'wolf'.

In the autumn, before United departed for the first leg of the World Club Championship in Buenos Aires against Estudiantes, Busby said, 'We do not want war.' Neither, it seemed, did the Argentinians. A party was arranged for the two teams the day before the game, so that they could fraternise. The United team drove 20 miles into town from their headquarters, only to discover after the party had been going half an hour that the Estudiantes players would not after all, be coming. It was said that their manager had stopped them, but there was the obvious suspicion that it had from the start been a move to disconcert United. Busby was furious, but refrained from comment and merely took his team straight back to their hotel.

Worse was to follow. In the programme notes for the match, Otto Gloria, manager of Benfica, had written by invitation that Stiles was 'brutal and a bad sportsman'. This was disgraceful on the part of the Estudiantes club, and succeeded in fanning the emotive pre-match comments in the Argentine press, which described Stiles as 'an assassin'. Two years after the World Cup in England, when Sir Alf Ramsey had called the Argentinians 'animals', feeling was still embittered. Not only was the whole of Buenos Aires gunning for Stiles, but the match officials too. During the game he was warned by the Uruguayan referee when a linesman claimed that he was standing 'too close' to an opponent—a new and hitherto unknown South American rule, it seemed.

This was ludicrous, for meanwhile certain Estudiantes players were committing the most outrageous fouls on United players; Bilardo and Pachame made scything attacks on Best and Charlton for which they should have been sent off. At one point, one of them kicked Dunne, then ran away as the free-kick was being taken, and with the referee watching the kick took the opportunity to punch

Best in the stomach as he passed. Some of the Argentinians had such crazed look in their eyes that a United player said afterwards: 'They looked as if they had been on drugs.'

Eventually came the inevitable: Stiles was sent off. Penalised for being off-side, a doubtful decision in itself, he waved his arm in disgust—and was promptly dismissed from the field. Busby's comment was: 'I would be the first to let Stiles know if I thought he should have been dismissed, but I felt very sorry for him, and have told him to forget about it.'

Estudiantes scored the only goal of the game after half an hour, Conigliaro heading in a corner by Vernon. Ten minutes later Sadler had a goal disallowed: United protested, but agreed afterwards, having seen the television film, that Foulkes had been off-side. Busby said in a mood of offended innocence: 'Holding the ball out there tonight put you in danger of your life.' This slight exaggeration was modified when he added: 'But you cannot stop playing these matches because of certain incidents. What better exponents of football have there been in the last 10 years than Brazil, and they are from South America. We can only solve these problems by playing more, not less.' It must be said that while the Estudiantes players went berserk, the crowd was unexceptional. Charlton said that he could not remember anything being thrown other than 'one bottle and a pound of mince'. Two-faced to the last, Estudiantes officials gave United a floral farewell, and before making a short speech, Louis Edwards, United's chairman, was asked what he had thought of their visit. 'Your hotel and your police were excellent,' he replied. To the English press he said: 'We shall continue to play in this competition if we get the chance because we want to be the best in the world.'

For the return leg United were moderately confident that if they kept their tempers they should be able to overcome a single-goal deficit. But at Old Trafford the Argentinians quickly showed that they could not only fight but play football. It had been the same with their national team in the World Cup—supremely talented and uniquely villainous. After five minutes Estudiantes doubled their lead with a goal from Veron, and it was only late in the game that

Morgan, signed from Burnley for £110,000, made it 1—2 on aggregate. Kidd forced the ball over the line for a second goal that would
have earned a play-off, but the whistle had already gone, and another
depressing chapter in this stormy competition was over. During the
game Law had been carried off, Charlton had a huge gash in his leg,
and Best and Medina were sent off. Only United's bank manager
could be pleased.

—13—
PASSING THE TORCH

The summer of 1968 was one of ultimate triumph for Matt Busby. The European Cup was finally won: knighted in June, there was little more left for him to achieve. An ambition to be the first British manager to win the World Club Championship had persuaded him to stay on, but there must have been considerable temptation for him to finish at the top. The club was in a healthy state—Champions of Europe with a team only two of which had cost large fees. Speculation about Busby's successor had been growing for some time, but at the Lord Mayor's reception in Manchester after winning at Wembley he had shown no signs of retiring when he said: 'Let us hope this is not the end, just the beginning.'

His resilience astonished younger men. Bill Shankly, manager of Liverpool, said before the start of the 1968–9 season: 'How he has carried on for so long I just don't know. When the beginning of each season comes, and you're wondering whether you should make changes, and whether they'll be right, whether the public will agree, the pressures are terrible. Matt must have the constitution of an ox.' The opportunities to relax are rare; always the manager is on call, at home or abroad.

So it was no surprise when, in January 1969, Busby announced that he was giving up the position of team manager, and would in future be general manager. After 23 years, during which time he had made a profit for the club of over £1 million, his energy was running down. He explained: 'I found I was not spending enough time with the team, and that is something you cannot afford. I now feel it is time for a younger man to come in. The trouble is, it is almost impossible for me to forget football for a minute of my waking life. I have it at meals, driving the car, socially. The only time I get a break is on the golf course. I can't even go to another match without there being speculation about who I've come to see.' Which, of course, some would say was reasonable enough.

In further explanation he said: 'For some time now, and certainly since our victory in the European Cup, I have been looking to the future. I feel it is time for someone in a track-suit to take over the players out on the training pitch. As it is, United have become more than just a football club, they are now an institution. I am finding less and less time to attend to the thing I consider paramount, which is the playing side.' As so many times, he had come to the decision quietly and logically. His wife Jean said: 'You know Matt. He is so calm, it has always been hard to measure the fires burning inside. But I would say his health has been good and he always sleeps well. Even so, when he told me his decision I didn't really believe it, though I knew it was in his mind. "It's got to be done, Jean," was all he said.'

The appointment of a team manager was to be delayed; the speculation increased. The position, with Busby still at Old Trafford as general manager, would need not only ability but tact and diplomacy. In the *Sunday Telegraph* I wrote an open letter to his successor:

'Unenviable Sir,

I think you will have both the best and the worst job in the game, for you are walking into a situation comparable to Arsenal after Chapman—you can hardly hope to do as well, following in the steps of one of the two greatest managers of the century. You inherit not only an incomparable tradition, but a struggling team [*as they were at the time*] in an era when almost all opponents have some joyless antidote to excellence and individualism, the qualities upon which that tradition has been built. Your job will be made both easier and more difficult because of the decision, not altogether wise in my opinion, that Sir Matt shall remain as general manager. You will be glad of his unrivalled experience, wisdom and diplomatic counsel, but inevitably you will be sometimes restricted and always overshadowed by his Olympian presence. It will be that much harder to establish the respect and command in your own right which he has enjoyed. It may well be, whatever your industry and leadership, whatever funds are at your disposal to acquire new players, that Manchester United are about to enter one of their leanest periods since the war. The great players, with the exception of Best, are slowing down, the existing youngsters seem to me to be short of former standards. The type of player you might hope to buy is increasingly rare, and, as with Mike England and Allan Clarke, you may fail to get them.

'The contemporary changes in tactics and finance have widened the gap between the good and the bad clubs but narrowed the margin among the good, to the point where it is almost impossible to be exceptional. Manchester United have always stood for entertainment and adventure, but these elements are being squeezed out of the game. In spite of this I hope that with the resources at your disposal you will try to provide entertaining as well as successful football whenever possible, and I hope too you will always be conscious of the good name not only of your illustrious club but of the game itself, eschewing those tactics and attitudes which debase everyone, a cancer which can kill the game. Manchester United are seen as leaders, not just in England but in the world. Everyone wishes you the best of luck in a job which will take the leasehold on your soul.'

During the next three months several names were discussed in the press as likely candidates for the job—Revie, Carey, Greenwood, Adamson, prominent managers of the moment. Then came the announcement which was in many ways expected: Wilf McGuinness was to be promoted from coach to chief coach. It was perhaps inevitable that Busby should decide—and none can doubt that it was his decision—to preserve the feeling of family that had existed at Old Trafford under his guidance. When needing men for the staff, the club had almost always turned to former players—Whalley, Aston, Crompton, and later, as coaches, McGuinness and Foulkes. It seems obvious that the qualities Busby most wanted in his successor were, besides ability as a coach, an understanding of how Manchester United had been built into a great club, and an already established loyalty to the cause. Continuity was more important than immediate prestige: with McGuinness there would be almost no interruption in the pattern of things. Some said McGuinness had been too closely associated with players still in the first team to have their respect, but he had been demanding this in training for several years.

He had, too, a combination of the contrasting qualities found in Busby himself—a certain charm, an easy way with people, yet a core of toughness which though only glimpsed occasionally by the outsider would be essential. If he lacked Busby's urbanity, that would come in time. When I went to interview him shortly after the appointment I offered him a cigar. 'No, thanks, I haven't got round to those yet,' he said with a slightly self-conscious smile, as if to accept would have in some ways been usurping Busby's seniority. Of the appointment Busby said: 'This is a sort of preliminary. All the great names in the game have started this way. He has a bit of experience to pick up yet in management. I think he will have enough to bite on with responsibility for the team, without taking on other things which could come later.' Unmistakably, the headmaster touch.

One story more than any other illustrates the kind of dedication McGuinness possessed. Shortly after he had joined the club as a boy, he was told by Jimmy Murphy during training that he must improve his right foot. Murphy got him hitting a ball against a wall, but was called away to the phone. Then there was another call, then someone to see him; by the time he returned almost an hour later, there was McGuinness still at work against the wall. As a schoolboy, Murphy recalled, McGuinness was 'ungainly, flat-footed and knock-kneed, and ran in a peculiar way, yet in spite of these disadvantages he became a highly successful player'. When Murphy tried to sign him, young McGuinness stalled; even Manchester United were not going to rush him into a decision. From an early age he knew his own mind, and was an obvious leader, captaining Manchester, Lancashire and England schoolboys. In 1957 Busby said of him:

'McGuinness is one of the most valuable players at Old Trafford because he always makes a habit of playing above himself when I promote him to the first team. Still only 19, Wilf is the sort of player every manager wants.' Within two years he twice played for England, before breaking his leg against Stoke Reserves on December 12, 1959. 'What you first noticed about him on the field was his aggression,' Joe Armstrong said. In the light of all this it is hardly surprising that Busby felt no need to go outside the club for a successor.

Having failed to make a sufficient recovery from his injury to continue as a professional, McGuinness had become a junior coach with United, and early in his new job was making his mark. 'I quickly learned that coaching of young players was not optional,' he said. 'They *must* be coached, just as actors must rehearse. Coaching is not a luxury but a necessity.' Already then, in the early sixties, intensive application of method was beginning to push some clubs ahead of United in the scramble for honours.

McGuinness succeeded Busby towards the end of a moderate season, in which United finished 11th in the League, beat Exeter, Watford and Birmingham in the F.A. Cup before losing to Everton 1—0 in the sixth round; and again reached the semi-final of the European Cup, following the dismal World Championship affair. Charlton had been made club captain in place of Law, whose personal struggle to regain fitness and a regular place disqualified him. For the third successive season Manchester United were watched at Old Trafford by more than a million spectators. Indeed, when United played Manchester City in a friendly cricket match, the game drew more spectators than the first day of the Old Trafford Test match. There might be a change at the helm, but the club's appeal remained magnetic.

They might well have retained the European Cup—Real Madrid, Benfica and Internazionale of Milan had previously achieved this—but for two dubious refereeing decisions in the semi-final against A.C. Milan. In the earlier rounds United had beaten Waterford from Ireland, Anderlecht, and Rapide of Vienna. After leading 3—0 at home to Anderlecht, there were visions of another Lisbon disaster when they struggled to hold out for 1—3 in the return. Confidence returned against Rapide; in the first leg, at home, they won 3—0 through Best (2) and Morgan, who scored on his European Cup début, and were equally impressive in the return, a goal-less draw, earning praise from Rudolf Vitlacyl, the former Czechoslovakian national manager now with Rapide: 'I was impressed by Manchester United's ability to attack away from home.' The old instinct was still there.

The first leg of the semi-final was played in Milan. A free-kick was given against Brennan, Foulkes went up to head clear, misjudged, and as the ball came down Sormani controlled it with his hand. The whole United defence stood still, waiting for a free-kick which never came, Sormani exploiting the situation to score. Then Fitzpatrick was sent off for retaliating against provocation by Hamrin, one of Sweden's stars in the 1958 World Cup Final which they lost to Brazil; Hamrin, escaping notice, scored Milan's second. With Best and Morgan shackled by Anquilletti and Schnellinger, United's attack spluttered fitfully. At Old Trafford they had the edge, but could not score until the 70th minute, when Charlton hit one of his specials from a chance beautifully made by Best. The crowd behaved deplorably, pelting Cudicini, Milan's 'keeper, with coins and rubbish; when, with 13 minutes to go, a chip from Crerand was scrambled over the line by Law, Anquilletti managed to shovel it away before the referee or linesman could give a goal. A minute late Kidd was just wide from a corner by Charlton and United were finished. In the final Milan were easy winners over Ajax of Holland; yet once more United had the frustration of knowing the fates had not smiled on them. Though only spasmodically touching their best form, they could have won the Cup, and so competed the next year: now it would be another two seasons or more before they could have another chance. Leeds were the new League Champions, a team of formidable consistency whose strength, organisation and application made them one of the most feared opponents in Europe. The next few years would really test McGuinness.

But what of Busby's future? Gradually he felt himself drifting apart from the team. Now it was he who had to court the friendship of the players; the respect was still there, but the intimacy, the feeling of a shared responsibility on the morning of a big match which is the emotional climax of the weekly cycle, was no longer his. He had moved 'upstairs', and was now slightly distant like one of the directors. You could sense that being removed from the heart of things left him uneasy.

Certainly, he could now spend more time with his family, could read the books of Russian and Spanish history which interested him but for which he had had no time during the past quarter of a century. He could sit back and take satisfaction from the material things his success had given him—a comfortable house in a pleasant Manchester suburb, a 150 m.p.h. Jensen car, the holidays in the sun which gave him the greatest relaxation of all. But this was not enough to satisfy a man who all his life had been at the hub of an organisation, making the decisions which were followed with interest by millions.

The obvious progression would be for the game to which he had given so much, in prestige and example, now to reward him with a position of authority in its national administration. The most civilised communities have always profited from the experience of their elders, yet the regulations of both the Football Association and the Football League forbade the election of professionals as officers—those best qualified to decide what is necessary off the field for the game they control on the field.

Instead, the League was governed by men who in many instances were incapable of running their own clubs, the Football Association congested with representatives of the amateur side of the game, many of whom had not spoken in council for 10 years, those who did often being ignorant of the real problems or bound by petty self-interest. The game had long cried out for men of world-wide professional experience to be co-opted, in order to guide the elected amateurs. Matt Busby, over 40 years a professional, was exactly the kind of man required—unemotional, balanced, a convincing speaker in any company, one to whom others warmed. His election as a vice-president, say, of the Football Association would immeasurably have increased the respect for Britain's voice in the troubled international sphere. The European F.A. had already given a lead by appointing him, in 1968, to their technical committee.

When Busby first began to make his mark as a manager at the start of the war, 30 years before, 'his was the voice that always carried the logic', recalled Joe Mercer. And so it continued to be. He sensed long in advance the rise of the continental threat. Having managed the British Olympic team in 1948 and then seen the bleeding of the Swedish and Danish teams—the gold and bronze medallists—by avaricious clubs from Italy, France and Germany, Busby campaigned more strongly than ever for the removal of the maximum wage. 'How otherwise can we hope to keep our best players, in the face of the temptation of huge wages with foreign clubs,' he argued. Before the freedom of wages, John Charles, Jimmy Greaves, Denis Law and Joe Baker were transferred abroad.

Busby led the argument for the greater protection of goal-keepers—'It would improve the game if they were free to use the ball intelligently'—and the introduction of substitutes; also for the streamlining of fixtures—though here he was motivated by the pressure of United's programme created by their success—and the reduction in staff by smaller clubs to balance their books; also for separate management committees of the different divisions, so that each could suit its own requirements. But never did he have any platform other than signed press articles. Now there existed the opportunity for him to be given access to the corridors of power: it was short-sighted that the opportunity was neglected. Furthermore, it encouraged him, damagingly as would become apparent, to remain too involved at Old Trafford. There were many signs that the game was becoming sick—the skill on which alone the game could survive being crushed by a permissive attitude to violence. At the start of the 1969—70 season Busby said in an interview with *The Observer*:

'The way things are going alarms me deeply. Hard men are nothing new in football. In my young days there were quite a few killers about, men who went in for rough play and intimidation. But you wouldn't expect one team to have more than a couple of them. What is new and frightening about the present situation is that you have entire sides that have physical hardness for their main asset. They use strength and fitness to neutralise skill, and the unfortunate truth is that all too often it can be done. Of course, there are really great players who cannot be subdued all the time, but their talents are seen only in flashes and they have to live dangerously. George Best survives only because his incredible balance allows him to ride with the impact of some of the tackles he has to take. Because of their heart and skill, he and other outstanding players in the League can go on giving the crowds entertainment. And it's true that there are still a few teams who believe the game is about talent and technique and imagination, but for any one, you'll find ten who rely on runners and hard men.'

You would never hear such straight talk from the men who govern football, because they are exclusively elected from within the game, and most have vested interests in individual clubs—other than the then secretaries of the F.A. and League, Denis Follows and Alan Hardaker, neither of whom had playing experience. The laws of the game are controlled by the International Board, which consists of one member each from England, Scotland, Northern Ireland and Wales, and four from F.I.F.A., representing the rest of the world. In other words, Britain has a half say in the laws throughout the world. Yet not one of the eight men with votes in Busby's time had any real playing experience, though Sir Stanley Rous, president of F.I.F.A., was a leading referee in his time. What better, then, than that Busby should have been England's, or Scotland's, spokesman on the International Board. Even at 61 he would still have been one of the Board's younger members, able to give the game possibly many years of valuable guidance.

To do so he would, of course, have had to relinquish his job as general manager of Manchester United, but once McGuinness had established himself securely this would have been possible without jeopardising the future of the club. Sooner or later the club would have to survive without him; there was no reason why he should not move on to apply his sanguine intelligence over a wider field. Only the jealousy of petty men in high places would prevent him.

The level of debate in the councils of the Football Association and Football League has usually been depressingly low. Matters of importance are often obscured rather than clarified by discussion. Busby, in any company, was always a compelling speaker. He had this gift of simplicity. While others become pompous or involved or heated, and use a manner of speech alien to their personality, Busby could put a large audience instantly at ease with a sincere informality which contained the telling impact of common sense. In particular there was his reply to the toast in his honour at a dinner given by the National Sporting Club in London. The assembled company was sophisticated, wealthy, educated, titled; there were some erudite preliminary speeches. When he rose to thank the club for honouring him, Busby struck exactly the right note of dignity, yet with a charm which in itself lifted him above the previous speakers. At the time, Manchester United had recently been involved in controversy on the field. He did not try to excuse them, but in a few words eloquently put the view that football in the sum of things was still more a benefit to the community than the evil which some believed it to be. He had a flair for putting events in the right perspective.

POSTSCRIPT

T hat sense of perspective, however, was partially to desert Busby in the years following his retirement as manager. Having taken the decision—unwisely some would say with hindsight and even at the time—to remain within the club which he had helped turn into a legend, Busby found it difficult, in a way he never had before, to distinguish what was in the best interests of the club. It was even more difficult for him to decide the extent to which he should bring to bear his influence on the course adopted by a succession of, in the event, relatively unsuccessful managers following in his wake. Not only the lustre and reputation he had helped create at the club—as with Arsenal and Herbert Chapman in the 30s—but the shadow of his own fame would make the task for anyone attempting to recreate a successful team more than ordinarily hazardous.

Whatever the soundness of the reasoning—the wish of Busby and the directors to retain within Old Trafford that sense of family and intimacy, the same as was to distinguish Liverpool's quarter of a century at the forefront of the game—behind the appointment of McGuinness, his reign was always bound to be controversial. Though disappointing for all concerned—no less for McGuinness, who 25 years later retains the same love of his club that he has cherished ever since he was a boy apprentice, than for United's huge audience—McGuinness was confronted by circumstances that doomed his prospects. It came as no real surprise when Busby relieved McGuinness of his duties during the 1969–70 season and himself returned to the helm. To have remained as general manager when appointing McGuinness was, as stated, an ill-judged decision.

McGuinness would never have the chance to establish that autocratic command, at the expense of even the directors, that had been the hallmark of Busby himself in his earliest days at Old Trafford.

McGuinness had known, as well if not better than anyone, that a new broom was needed at Old Trafford and that it would have to be used vigorously. Yet as a former player attempting to direct men, some of them household names, who were once his colleagues—not to say superiors, he found himself in an impossible position. Disgruntled players took their grievances to Busby, over McGuinness's head. He had huge responsibility, but, it became increasingly apparent, no ultimate authority. He had been given the job, it is not an exaggeration to say, not just because he was an energetic, developing coach who had proved himself with young players and was devoted to the club, but because Busby basically mistrusted anyone from outside Old Trafford. What Busby had failed to understand, it became increasingly apparent, was the extent to which the levels of discipline and dedication among the players, which he himself had once inspired until it had reached a point at which he could take these qualities for granted, had declined during the latter years of his own management, to such a degree that Manchester United was heading for serious trouble some time before McGuinness was appointed to restore the glory.

It had been Bobby Charlton's opinion at the time United achieved Busby's dream of winning the European Cup in 1968 that the team was no longer as good as it had been. Writing on his own retirement in 1973, Charlton said: 'It wasn't a strong side really (1968), not at all. But when Sir Matt, who'd been knighted that year, decided to retire from team managing in 1969, I didn't actually feel that we were on the edge of a crisis, even though he had already ceased to be involved with the team physically, in training, and we'd seen less and less of him. By the end, he hardly came to training at all. Things hadn't exactly got slack. Jack Crompton, the trainer, did a good job. But things *had* changed. It got to the stage where you had to build yourself up mentally, at least I know that *I* was having to. . . . As Sir Matt receded from day-to-day things, the influence of his personality had decreased. As young players came into the team they weren't exposed to his influence. Things had dwindled over a period of years. I think McGuinness was chosen because the club had always had this family feeling, and the board were frightened that someone from outside would make too many sweeping changes. Who knows, maybe that's what was needed.'

It was. It required someone more mature and established than the eager but unfortunate McGuinness to dictate not only declining star figures such as Charlton and Law and the wayward Best, but Busby himself. It was soon clear to McGuinness that his responsibilities, beyond training, were imprecise. He was, for instance, not in control of contracts, which provide one of the means by which a manager can control a player, psychologically as well as factually. Yet McGuinness discovered that Law was being paid more than Charlton, that several were being paid more than himself, and that rifts in the squad were rife. It also became apparent to the new young manager that if players were to be bought, Busby's would remain the guiding hand. McGuinness was in charge of a team he could not wholly shape.

There was another, more subtle reason for the slide in Manchester United's fortunes. The game as it had existed at Old Trafford for 25 years, the game that had been created in Busby's fashion, was radically changing. The flow and spontaneity that had characterised the four great teams developed by Busby at different times was now being challenged; indeed, it had become a numbers game planned on a blackboard, a game in which flair and imagination were being squeezed out. As Charlton said, it was becoming more tactical; the younger players took longer to learn to read the game, whatever their technical skills, so they could not be introduced so early into the team. McGuinness was well aware of this shift in emphasis, was aware that United needed to introduce more tactical discipline, never mind the more subtle disciplines affecting morale off the field.

He could point, with moderate satisfaction, to the fact that at the end of his first season the team had finished eighth in the League and reached the semi-final of both F.A. and League Cups. That summer his title was elevated from that of 'coach' to 'manager', but by Christmas he was sacked, following defeat in the League Cup semi-final

by Aston Villa. The directors, guided by Busby, had become too conscious that the dressing room was in turmoil, never mind that
McGuinness had never been given the proper scope to make otherwise. With the ageing Busby once again at the helm, the United team,
though still ill at ease on and off the field, once more finished eighth in
the League; respectable enough for any club but this.

After delay and rumours, Frank O'Farrell was appointed manager
for the start of the following season. This pleasant, truthful and
stern man who had learnt the game with West Ham and Preston,
then as manager with Weymouth, Torquay and Leicester, was seen
as the right kind of figure to bring United back on course. He had
taken Leicester to promotion, and many within the game who knew
O'Farrell as firm but fair considered that he would be able to handle
the complex problems awaiting him. Yet on arrival at Old Trafford,
the Irishman discovered similar confusions about his responsibilities
just as had McGuinness. Busby had now become a director, while
Louis Edwards, a prominent wholesale butcher, had become chairman after a lengthy and expensive process of share accumulation.
O'Farrell had been wooed with a five-figure salary, substantial for
that time, but, disconcertingly, discovered that Busby still occupied
the manager's office on the club's first floor. Grasping this first unexpected nettle, he successfully demanded that the situation be
changed. The first stone of his foundation was already loose.

Whereas McGuinness, with little choice in the matter, had found
his status as manager was undermined by the fact that, while he was
busy in a tracksuit getting himself muddy directing affairs on the
training pitch, Busby was still running the club back at his office,
O'Farrell made the reverse mistake. He decided that he needed to be
closer to the administrative seat of power, spending much of his time
in a three-piece blue suit and stiff collar—almost a throwback to the
thirties—while training was left in the hands of his able assistant
Malcolm Musgrove, a former West Ham winger who had worked
with him at Leicester. Musgrove, like McGuinness, was one of the
new school of coaches, though by no means averse to the attacking game on which United's reputation traditionally stood. But, in
the eyes of some of United's senior players, who was Malcolm

Musgrove? There were too many fronts on which any new manager at Old Trafford had to fight, and a basic aspect of O'Farrell's policy meant that in the area of player-relations, always vital and never more so than in this interim phase of United's history, he was damagingly distancing himself from the heart of the matter.

Although the problems confronting O'Farrell were inherited, it would be debated at the time, and subsequently, whether he adopted the right lines in the attempt to correct them. Initially, all seemed well enough, and indeed by December in his first season O'Farrell's team led the League by five points. The position was to prove illusory, created as much as anything by the genius of Best, whose scintillating form throughout the autumn more than compensated for the mounting inadequacies that surrounded him on the field. These were soon to be surpassed by Best's own inadequacies; or, perhaps it should rather be said, frailties. This additional and complex problem, that of Best's failure to cope with the turmoils of his private life and the burden of his own fame, was to prove a nightmare for O'Farrell and one that, in conjunction with others, was to cause his downfall. His inability to control Best's increasingly wayward behaviour off the field magnified the frictions among the rest of the players. Unreasonable though that may have been—since on the field Best was helping them to earn their wages—the other players considered that O'Farrell's seeming leniency towards the excesses of the greatest talent ever seen in Britain was unacceptable. The early success evaporated, and before O'Farrell could come to terms with the legacy of fragmentation throughout the club, United were heading for relegation.

With hindsight, it was apparent that Best's phenomenal form in the autumn of 1971 merely served to postpone O'Farrell's ultimate crisis for 12 months. The successful run had turned on New Year's Day, with defeat at West Ham; and a 5—1 thrashing by Leeds at Elland Road raised doubts in the minds of Busby and Edwards about whether they had made the right choice. In March 1972, with Busby's apparent approval, O'Farrell attempted to buy himself out of trouble, signing Martin Buchan, the Scotland centre-back, for £130,000 and Ian Moore from Nottingham Forest for £200,000.

On the surface, at least, the new manager still had Busby's backing; though information began to seep out from within the club that Busby was unhappy with the defensive role given by O'Farrell—or, the cynics said, by Musgrove—to attacking players, to compensate for the team's poor defensive qualities. The dressing room, not least Charlton, was known to be unhappy with much of Musgrove's coaching, and indiscreet comments by Busby to close friends, leaked within Manchester, not only undermined O'Farrell, but led to increasing attacks in the press upon Busby, so recently a hero who had been considered immune to criticism. Now it was widely being said that Busby was helping to discredit the second man he had appointed in the hope that he would emulate him. O'Farrell furthered the doubts about the extent of his own command when, attempting to discipline Best for yet one more indiscretion, he sent the offending player before the board for an additional reprimand. The board fuelled public criticism of their behaviour, and Busby's, when suspending David Meek, the local correspondent of the *Manchester Evening News*, from travelling with the team—which he had done for the past 14 years—for stating that the board should express public confidence in the manager. More than ever it was now apparent that it was not a team that O'Farrell had needed to rebuild but a club. O'Farrell, on the other hand, had continued to misread the technical side of the dressing room, creating an imbalance of attacking players at a time when the priority was strengthening the defence. Morale within the club at all levels had reached an all-time post-war low.

'Maybe we didn't have the players,' Charlton said, following O'Farrell's eventual and inevitable dismissal. 'But there was no feeling of *fun* in the club anymore. The spirit was not helped by all the trouble with George Best. Three or four times O'Farrell let him off when the rest of the players were looking for a lead. . . . If you don't have a club that's happy, you've had it in the First Division. If you get this situation, and you come to an important match and ask the players for 100 per cent, they won't give it. Not deliberately, it's just something inside you. Believe me, the players were all for the *club*, even if they 'd lost faith in O'Farrell, but the Best business was an embarrassment to them. It seemed at times that George *was* the club. The atmosphere was terrible.'

It was no secret of this era that Bobby and George did not see eye to eye, the older player being intolerant, with some justification, of the other's irresponsibility. It may have been an extreme case that faced O'Farrell, involving a wayward national idol, but he significantly failed to resolve it. Furthermore, the resentment within the dressing room of this failure was swiftly passed first-hand to Busby on the golf course by Alex Stepney and Willie Morgan, with whom he regularly played golf. O'Farrell may have had no chance of obtaining a direct open line to his chairman, Edwards, who was never anything other than Busby's biggest fan. Edwards's arrival as chairman unavoidably ensured that, for better or worse, Busby's would remain the determining influence on most of what happened at Old Trafford for much of the seventies.

Sadly, O'Farrell's departure was conducted with anything but dignity, the club quibbling over his pay-off, as United faced the Christmas of 1972 with the serious possibility of relegation. On December 22 Tommy Docherty, as opposite a figure from O'Farrell as it was possible to find, was appointed in succession, having obtained release from his position as national manager from the Scottish Football Association. George Graham was bought from Arsenal for £120,000 and relegation was avoided, with the team finishing in 18th place. The problems, however, had not gone away. By the end of the season Charlton and Law had played their last games for United, and the following season relegation proved a reality. Such, however, was the continuing thirst for the game at Old Trafford, and Docherty's ability to produce positive football, that United's single season in the second division, 1974–5, produced an astonishing average attendance of 48,388.

George Best, having been leading scorer for five consecutive years from 1968 to 1972, was long gone and the leading scorer now was Stuart Pearson with 17, Gerry Daly and Lou Macari both scoring 11. A new era had arrived. Docherty's panache off the field, and his team's vivacity on the field, gradually reduced the relevance of the legendary figure in the boardroom to the playing affairs of the club.

The arrival of Steve Coppell from Tranmere Rovers for a mere £40,000 and, in 1976, Gordon Hill from Millwall for £70,000, were to help give United the excitement on the wings for which their spectators longed. Docherty's credibility, never mind the usual various indiscretions behind the scenes, publicly remained high. In a thrilling F.A. Cup final in 1976 United lost to Arsenal, and the following year won the Cup by defeating Liverpool, gaining United's first trophy since the European Cup. Yet barely a month later Docherty had gone, dismissed following a highly-publicized affair with the wife of the club's physiotherapist.

Now came Dave Sexton: a quiet, discreet manager more in the Busby mould. Yet if Sexton's appointment carried Busby's tacit approval, from here onwards Busby's power within the club was in decline. His disapproval of certain administrative decisions was ignored, and while Edwards's son Martin joined the board—eventually to become chairman and chief executive—an earlier agreement between Busby and Edwards that Busby's son Sandy should likewise join the board was not honoured. Although for four seasons Sexton's teams were attractive enough, they failed to achieve the most important prize of all, the League title. Sexton was said not to be able to 'communicate' with the public, to give the club an up-front public relations image that was felt appropriate, and in 1981 he was replaced by Ron Atkinson, a man who finds it difficult to be anything but up-front. Though Atkinson was twice to lead United to F.A. Cup victories, he too fell short of the elusive League ambition. Busby, meanwhile, had left the board and become club president, a revered figure whose magnetic charm and uncanny wisdom about the game's essential virtues continued to touch all those with the good fortune to meet him. It would take Alex Ferguson, appointed in November 1986, a further seven years to recapture the League title, and happily the Grand Old Man, who had done so much to make Manchester United the club it is, was there to see it happen.

With one of those strokes of fortune, Ferguson's signing of the discontented Cantona from Leeds, during the 1992-3 season, gave to his side at Old Trafford the catalyst for a new chemistry. Cantona was an echo of Viollet, from Busby's golden years; a player of positional instinct and awareness of others, with such ball control, such a feathery touch that suddenly the pieces of United's team found fresh harmony and opposing teams began to fall apart. With Giggs and Sharpe or Kanchelskis rampant on the wings, and Hughes finding his own game lifted alongside Cantona, the qualities on the field in search of which Busby had spent a lifetime were now once more in full flood.

Though pride was never evident in Busby, the restoration of Manchester United's special appeal must have warmed his ageing heart, and brought a quiet satisfaction to a man now lonely after the death, a few years before, of his dear Jean. Near to the end of his autumn years, the joy that United were once more bringing to a public that extended far beyond the boundaries of Manchester must have given reassurance, little though he would need it, that he had given his life worthily. What made Busby, a miner's son, one of the most admired men of his age was not his success, but his reaction to it. Success, he recognised early, is transitory; like a lighthouse he shone brightest when the storm was black. Bill Foulkes, who had played and worked with him for many years, the captain whose rare goal in Madrid had opened they way to the European Cup Final in 1968, once said to me: 'You know that poem *If* by Kipling. Of all the men I've met, I think Matt is that kind of fellow.' Sir Matthew Busby, father of modern football, had indeed come close to Kipling's paragon . . .

If . . .

If you can keep your head when all about you
Are losing theirs, and blaming it on you,
If you can trust yourself when all men doubt you
But make allowance for their doubting too;
If you can wait and not be tired by waiting,
Or being lied about, don't deal in lies,
Or being hated, don't give way to hating,
And yet don't look too good or talk too wise;
If you can dream—and not make dreams your master;
If you can think—and not make thoughts your aim;

If you can meet with triumph and disaster
And treat those two impostors just the same;
If you can bear to hear the truth you've spoken
Twisted by knaves to make a trap for fools,
Or watch the things you gave your life to, broken,
And stop and build 'em up with worn-out tools:
If you can make one heap of all your winnings
And risk it on one turn of pitch and toss
And lose, and start again at your beginnings
And never breathe a word about your loss;
If you can force your heart and nerve and sinew
To serve your turn long after they are gone,
And so hold on when there is nothing in you
Except the Will which says to them: Hold on;
If you can talk with crowds and keep your virtue
Or walk with kings—nor lose the common touch,
If neither foes nor loving friends can hurt you,
If all men count with you, but none too much;
If you can fill the unforgiving minute
with sixty seconds' worth of distance run,
Yours is the earth and everything that's in it,
And—which is more—you'll be a man, my son.

Rudyard Kipling [1865–1936]

APPENDIX I

FOUNDED: 1878. Elected to Football League: 1892

EUROPEAN CUP: Winners 1968; Semi-finalists 1957, 1958, 1966, 1969

WORLD CLUB CHAMPIONSHIP: Finalists 1968

FIRST DIVISION: Champions 1908, 1911, 1952, 1956, 1957, 1965, 1967; Runners-up 1947, 1948, 1951, 1959, 1964, 1968

SECOND DIVISION: Champions 1936; Runners-up 1897, 1906, 1935, 1938

F.A. CUP: Winners 1909, 1948, 1963; Finalists 1957, 1958; Semi-finalists 1909, 1926, 1949, 1962, 1964, 1965, 1966, 1970

FOOTBALL LEAGUE CUP: Semi-finalists 1970

F.A. CHARITY SHIELD: Winners 1908, 1911, 1952, 1957, 1958

F.A. YOUTH CUP: Winners 1953, 1954, 1955, 1956, 1957, 1964

FAIRS CUP: Semi-finalists 1965

HIGHEST ATTENDANCE: 76,962 Wolves *v.* Grimsby, F.A. Cup semi-final 1939

RECORD VICTORY: 10—0 *v.* Anderlecht, European Cup 1956

WORST DEFEAT: 0—7 *v.* Aston Villa, First Division 1930

MOST GOALS: 103 in 1957 (1st) and 1959 (2nd), 102 in 1960 (7th)

HIGHEST SCORER IN A SEASON: Denis Viollet, 32 in 1959–60

RECORD LEAGUE APPEARANCES: Bill Foulkes 563, Joe Spence 481

FOOTBALL LEAGUE

DIVISION I

Season	P	W	D	L	F	A	Pts	Position
1892–93	30	6	6	18	50	85	18	16th
1893–94	30	6	2	22	36	72	14	16th

DIVISION II

Season	P	W	D	L	F	A	Pts	Position
1894–95	30	15	8	7	78	44	38	3rd
1895–96	30	15	3	12	66	57	33	6th
1896–97	30	17	5	8	56	34	39	2nd

1897–98	30	16	6	8	64	35	38	4th
1898–99	34	19	5	10	67	43	43	4th
1899–1900	34	20	4	10	63	27	44	4th
1900–01	34	14	4	16	42	38	32	10th
1901–02	34	11	6	17	38	53	28	15th
1902–03	34	15	8	11	53	38	38	5th
1903–04	34	20	8	6	65	33	48	3rd
1904–05	34	24	5	5	81	30	53	3rd
1905–06	38	28	6	4	90	28	62	2nd

DIVISION I

1906–07	38	17	8	13	53	56	42	8th
1907–08	38	23	6	9	81	48	52	Champions
1908–09	38	15	7	16	58	68	37	13th
1909–10	38	19	7	12	69	61	45	5th
1910–11	38	22	8	8	72	40	52	Champions
1911–12	38	13	11	14	45	60	37	13th
1912–13	38	19	8	11	69	43	46	4th
1913–14	38	15	6	17	52	62	36	14th
1914–15	38	9	12	17	46	62	30	18th
1919–20	42	13	14	15	54	50	40	12th
1920–21	42	15	10	17	64	68	40	13th
1921–22	42	8	12	22	41	73	28	22nd

DIVISION II

1922–23	42	17	14	11	51	36	48	4th
1923–24	42	13	14	15	52	44	40	14th
1924–25	42	23	11	8	57	23	57	2nd

DIVISION I

1925–26	42	19	6	17	66	73	44	9th
1926–27	42	13	14	15	52	64	40	15th
1927–28	42	16	7	19	72	80	39	18th
1928–29	42	14	13	15	66	76	41	12th
1929–30	42	15	8	19	67	88	38	17th
1930–31	42	7	8	27	53	115	22	22nd

172

DIVISION II

1931–32	42	17	8	17	71	72	42	12th
1932–33	42	15	13	14	71	68	43	6th
1933–34	42	14	6	22	59	85	34	20th
1934–35	42	23	4	15	76	55	50	5th
1935–36	42	22	12	8	85	43	56	1st

DIVISION I

1936–37	42	10	12	20	55	78	32	21st

DIVISION II

1937–38	42	22	9	11	82	50	53	2nd

DIVISION I

1938–39	42	11	16	15	57	65	38	14th

Busby Appointed

1946–47	42	22	12	8	95	54	56	2nd
1947–48	42	19	14	9	81	48	52	2nd
1948–49	42	21	11	10	77	44	53	2nd
1949–50	42	18	14	10	69	44	50	4th
1950–51	42	24	8	10	74	40	56	2nd
1951–52	42	23	11	8	95	52	57	Champions
1952–53	42	18	10	14	69	72	46	8th
1953–54	42	18	12	12	73	38	48	4th
1954–55	42	20	7	15	84	74	47	5th
1955–56	42	25	10	7	83	51	60	Champions
1956–57	42	28	8	6	103	54	64	Champions
1957–58	42	16	11	15	85	75	43	9th
1958–59	42	24	7	11	103	66	55	2nd
1959–60	42	19	7	16	102	80	45	7th
1960–61	42	18	9	15	88	76	45	7th
1961–62	42	15	9	18	72	75	39	15th
1962–63	42	12	10	20	67	81	34	19th
1963–64	42	23	7	12	90	62	53	2nd
1964–65	42	26	9	7	89	39	61	Champions

1965–66	42	18	15	9	84	59	41	4th
1966–67	42	24	12	6	84	45	60	Champions
1967–68	42	24	8	10	89	55	56	2nd
1968–69	42	15	12	15	57	53	42	11th
1969–70	42	14	17	11	66	61	45	8th
1970–71	42	16	11	15	65	66	43	8th

LEADING LEAGUE SCORERS

1946–47	Jack Rowley 26
1947–48	Jack Rowley 23
1948–49	Jack Rowley 20
1949–50	Jack Rowley 20
1950–51	Stan Pearson 18
1951–52	Jack Rowley 30
1952–53	Stan Pearson 16
1953–54	Tommy Taylor 22
1954–55	Tommy Taylor 20
	Denis Viollet 20
1955–56	Tommy Taylor 20
1956–57	Bill Whelan 26
1957–58	Denis Viollet 17

1958–59	Bobby Charlton 29
1959–60	Denis Viollet 32
	(club record)
1960–61	Bobby Charlton 21
1961–62	David Herd 14
1962–63	Denis Law 23
1963–64	Denis Law 30
1964–65	Denis Law 28
1965–66	David Herd 24
1966–67	Denis Law 23
1967–68	George Best 28
1968–69	George Best 19
1969–70	George Best 15

F.A. CUP RECORD UNDER BUSBY

1947 3R: Bradford 3—0 (A); 4R: Nottingham Forest 0—2 (H)

1948 3R: Aston Villa 6—4 (A); 4R: Liverpool 3—0 (H);
5R: Charlton 2—0 (H); 6R: Preston 4—1 (H); SF:
Derby 3—1 (Hillsborough); F: Blackpool 4—2

1949 3R: Bournemouth 6—0 (H); 4R: Bradford 1—1, 1—1, 5—0;
5R: Yeovil 8—0 (H); 6R: Hull 1—0 (A); SF: Wolves 1—1
(Hillsborough), 0—1 (Goodison)

1950 3R: Weymouth 4—0 (H); 4R: Watford 1—0 (A); 5R:
Portsmouth 3—3 (H), 3—1 (A); 6R: Chelsea 0—2 (A)

1951 3R: Oldham 4—1 (H); 4R: Leeds 4—0 (H);
5R: Arsenal 1—0 (H); 6R: Birmingham 0—1 (A)

1952 3R: Hull 0—2 (H)

1953 3R: Millwall 1—0 (A); 4R: Walthamstow 1—1 (H), 5—2

(A); 5R: Everton 1—2 (A)

1954 3R: Burnley 3—5 (A)

1955 3R: Reading 1—1, 4—1, 4R: Manchester City 0—2 (A)

1956 3R: Bristol Rovers 0—4 (A)

1957 3R: Hartlepools 4—3 (A); 4R: Wrexham 5—0 (A);
5R: Everton 1—0 (H); 6R: Bournemouth 2—1 (A);
SF: Birmingham 2—0 (Hillsborough); F: Aston Villa 1—2

1958 3R: Workington 3—1 (A); 4R: Ipswich 2—0 (H); 5R:
Sheffield Wednesday 3—0 (H); 6R: W.B.A. 2—2 (A), 1—0
(H); SF: Fulham 2—2 (Villa Park), 5—3 (Highbury);
F: Bolton 0—2

1959 3R: Norwich 0—3 (A)

1960 3R: Derby 4—2 (A); 4R: Liverpool 3—1 (A); 5R: Sheffield
Wednesday 0—1 (H)

1961 3R: Middlesbrough 3—0 (H); 4R: Sheffield Wednesday 1—1
(A), 2—7 (H)

1962 3R: Bolton 2—1 (H); 4R: Arsenal 1—0 (H); 5R: Sheffield
Wednesday 0—0 (H), 2—0 (A); 6R: Preston 0—0 (A), 2—1
(H); SF: Spurs 1—3 (Hillsborough)

1963 3R: Huddersfield 5—0 (H), 4R: Aston Villa 1—0 (H);
5R: Chelsea 2—1 (H); 6R: Coventry 3—1 (A);
SF: Southampton (Villa Park) 1—0; F: Leicester 3—1

1964 3R: Southampton 3—2 (A); 4R: Bristol Rovers 4—1 (H);
5R: Barnsley 4—0 (A); 6R: Sunderland 3—3 (H), 2—2 (A),
5—1 (Huddersfield); SF: West Ham 1—3 (Hillsborough)

1965 3R: Chester 2—1 (H); 4R: Stoke 0—0 (A), 1—0 (H);
5R: Burnley 2—1 (H); 6R: Wolves 5—3 (A); SF: Leeds 0—0
(Hillsborough), 0—1 (Nottingham)

1966 3R: Derby 5—2 (A); 4R: Rotherham 0—0 (H), 1—0 (A);
5R: Wolves 4—2 (A); 6R: Preston 1—1 (A), 3—1 (H);
SF: Everton 0—1 (Bolton)

1967 3R: Stoke 2—0 (H); 4R: Norwich 1—2 (H)

1968 3R: Spurs 2—2 (H), 0—1 (A)

1969 3R: Exeter 3—1 (A); 4R: Watford 1—1 (H), 2—0 (A);
5R: Birmingham 2—2 (A), 6—2 (H); 6R: Everton 0—1 (H)

1970 3R: Ipswich 1—0 (A); 4R: Manchester City 3—0 (H);
      5R: Northampton 8—2 (A); 6R: Middlesbrough 1—1 (A),
      2—1 (H); SF: Leeds 0—0 (Hillsborough), 0—0 (Villa Park),
      0—1 (Burnden Park)
1970 3R: Middlesbrough 0—0 (H), 1—2 (A)

EUROPEAN CUP RESULTS
1956–57
1. Anderlecht (Belgium) 2—0 (A), 10—0 (H)
2. Borussia Dortmund (W. Germany) 3—2 (H), 0—0 (A)
QF. Bilbao (Spain) 3—5 (A), 3—0 (H)
SF. Real Madrid (Spain) 1—3 (A), 2—2 (H)

1957–58
1. Shamrock Rovers (Eire) 6—0 (A), 3—2 (H)
2. Dukla (Czechoslovakia) 3—0 (H), 0—1 (A)
QF. Red Star Belgrade (Yugoslavia) 2—1 (H), 3—3 (A)
SF. AC Milan (Italy) 2—1 (H), 0—4 (A)

1965–66
1. Helsinki HIK (Finland) 3—2 (A), 6—0 (H)
2. ASK Vorvaerts (E. Germany) 2—0 (A), 3—1 (H)
QF. Benfica (Portugal) 3—2 (H), 5—1 (A)
SF. Partizan Belgrade (Yugoslavia) 0—2 (A), 1—0 (H)

1967–68
1. Hibernian (Malta) 4—0 (H), 0—0 (A)
2. Sarajevo (Yugoslavia) 0—0 (A), 2—1 (H)
QF. Gornick (Poland) 2—0 (H), 0—1 (A)
SF. Real Madrid (Spain) 1—0 (H), 3—3 (A)
F. Benfica (Portugal) at Wembley 4—1 after extra time

1968–69
1. Waterford (Eire) 3—1 (A), 7—1 (H)
2. Anderlecht (Belgium) 3—0 (H), 1—3 (A)
QF. Rapide Vienna (Austria) 3—0 (H), 0—0 (A)

SF. AC Milan (Italy) 0—2 (A), 1—0 (H)

EUROPEAN CUP APPEARANCES
Foulkes 35; Charlton 28; Crerand 24; Tony Dunne, Stiles 23; Best 21; Law 18; Kidd 16; Stepney 15; Bryne, Sadler, Tommy Taylor 14; Colman 13; Edwards, Pegg, Viollet, Wood 12; Berry, Brennan, Whelan 11; Jones 10; Burns, Gregg 9; Aston, Connelly, Herd 8; Fitzpatrick 7; Morgan 6; Blanchflower, Webster 5; Morgans 4; Cantwell, Goodwin, Scanlon 3; Cope, Crowther, Pat Dunne, Greaves, James, McGuinness, Mark Pearson, Rimmer, Ryan, Sartori, Ernie Taylor 2; Anderson, Gaskell, Kopel 1.

EUROPEAN CUP GOALS
Law 14; Viollet 13; Tommy Taylor 11; Best, Charlton 10; Connelly 6; Herd, Whelan 5; Pegg 4; Berry, Kidd, Sadler 3; Foulkes, Morgan 2; Aston, Burns, Colman, Crerand, Sartori, Stiles, Ernie Taylor, Webster 1; own goals 2.

EUROPEAN CUP-WINNERS Cup
1963–64
1. Willem II (Holland) 1—1 (A), 6—1 (H)
2. Spurs (England) 0—2 (A), 4—1 (H)
QF. Sporting Lisbon (Portugal) 4—1 (H), 0—5 (A)

INTER-CITIES FAIRS' CUP
1964–65
1. Djurgaardens (Sweden) 1—1 (A), 6—1 (H)
2. Borussia Dortmund (W. Germany) 6—1 (A), 4—0 (H)
3. Everton (England) 1—1 (H), 2—1 (A)
QF. Racing Strasbourg (France) 5—0 (A), 0—0 (H)
SF. Ferencvaros (Hungary) 3—2 (H), 0—1 (A), 1—2 (A)
   (Budapest)

FOOTBALL LEAGUE CUP
1960–61 Exeter 1—1 (A), 4—1 (H); Bradford City 1—2 (A)
1966–67 Blackpool 1—5 (A)

1969–70 Middlesbrough 1—0 (H); Wrexham 2—0 (H); Burnley
          0—0 (A); 1—0 (H); Derby 0—0 (A), 1—0 (H); SF:
          Manchester City 1—2 (A), 2—2 (H)

1970–71 Aldershot 3—1 (A); Portsmouth 1—0 (H); Chelsea
          2—1 (H); Crystal Palace 4—2 (H); Aston Villa 0—0 (H),
          1—2 (A)

APPENDIX II

THOSE WHO DIED

PLAYERS

Roger Byrne (left-back), Geoff Bent (reserve left-back), Eddie Colman (right-half), Mark Jones (centre-half), Duncan Edwards (left-half), Bill Whelan (inside-right), Tommy Taylor (centre-forward), David Pegg (outside-left).

JOURNALISTS

Alf Clarke (*Manchester Evening Chronicle*), Don Davies (*Manchester Guardian*), George Follows (*Daily Herald*), Tom Jackson (*Manchester Evening News*), Archie Ledbrooke (*Daily Mirror*), Henry Rose (*Daily Express*), Frank Swift (*News of the World*), Eric Thompson (*Daily Mail*).

CLUB OFFICIALS

Walter Crickmer (secretary), Tom Curry (trainer), Bert Whalley (coach).

CREW

Captain K. G. Rayment (co-pilot), W. T. Cable (steward).

OTHERS

B. P. Miklos (travel agent), Willie Satinoff (supporter and race-horse owner).

THE SURVIVORS

Matt Busby (Manchester United manager)

PLAYERS

Johnny Berry (outside-right), Jackie Blanchflower (centre-half), Bobby Charlton (inside-left), Bill Foulkes (right-back), Harry Gregg (goal-keeper), Ken Morgans (outside-right), Albert Scanlon (outside-left), Denis Viollet (inside-left), Ray Wood (goal-keeper).

PRESS
Ted Ellyard (*Daily Mail* photographer), Peter Howard (*Daily Mail* photographer), Frank Taylor (*News Chronicle*).

CREW
Captain J. Thain (pilot), G. Rodgers (radio officer), Margaret Bellis (stewardess), Rosemary Cheverton (stewardess).

OTHERS
Mrs. Vera Lukic and baby, Mrs. B. P. Miklos, N. Tomasevic.

APPENDIX III

FROM THE *Daily Telegraph* OF JUNE 9, 1969:
Captain James Thain, 47, has been cleared of blame for the Munich air disaster on Feb. 6, 1958, in which 23 people were killed, including eight members of the Manchester United football team. Mr. Rodgers, Minister of State, Board of Trade, is expected to announce in the Commons tomorrow publication of the Government independent inquiry's findings on the crash, by Mr. Edgar Fay, Q.C. These uphold Captain Thain's contention that runway slush to a depth he could not have known, prevented the B.E.A. Elizabethan from taking off successfully. . . . Asked if, after more than a decade fighting to clear his name, he would try to fly again, he [Captain Thain] said: 'It is something only B.E.A. can answer. I love flying and I always will.' He said a great deal depended on exactly what the inquiry's report said. 'B.E.A. may find they have terminated my contract unjustly, in which case the first move might come from them.'

But B.E.A. held out little hope that Captain Thain, 36 at the time of the crash, would be offered back his job. A spokesman said: 'He was dismissed because he breached B.E.A.'s regulations by sitting in the wrong pilot's seat for take-off and for not inspecting the wings for ice.'

Mr. E. S. Fay, Q.C., was chairman of an inquiry in 1959–60 with different terms of reference which found that Captain Thain had 'departed with some snow on his wings'. The terms of reference for the new inquiry by Mr. Fay and two assessors were to find whether Captain Thain was to blame for the crash. Two German inquiries blamed him on the grounds that take-off was prevented by wing ice which he should have removed. Tests by Government scientists in 1965 showed conclusively that slush only half an inch deep could double take-off distance, and slush an inch or so deep could prevent take-off altogether. Until then it was generally believed that planes could take off in two inches of slush.

FROM *The Times* OF JUNE 11, 1969:

The key witness in the inquiry whose report yesterday cleared Captain James Thain from blame for the 1958 Munich air disaster, which killed 23 people, was a German pilot who was at Munich airport on the day of the crash. Herr Reinhard Meyer, a pilot since 1940 and an aircraft designer, was one of the first to reach the crashed aircraft. He told the British inquiry under Mr. E. S. Fay that he 'was thinking about possible reasons for it and . . . was considering whether aircraft icing could have been the reason'. He said there was nothing like frost or frozen deposit on the wings of the B.E.A. Elizabethan airliner as it lay at the end of the runway. 'There was melting snow only.'

The Ray Report comments: '. . . Herr Meyer was the only person to investigate the icing question within a short time of the accident. He looked with the eye of an experienced pilot and aircraft designer.' The inquiry finds that the cause of the crash was slush on the runway, and that it is 'possible but unlikely' that wing icing was a contributory cause.

Other findings of the inquiry, set up by the Prime Minister and the President of the Board of Trade in April last year, are that Captain Thain was not at fault with regard to runway slush, but that he was at fault with regard to wing icing. 'But', the report adds, 'because wing icing is unlikely to have been a contributory cause of the accident, blame cannot be imputed to him.' The report also finds that Captain Thain, now aged 48 and a smallholder in Berkshire, was at fault in permitting his co-pilot — another captain — to occupy the left instead of the right-hand seat, 'but this played no part in causing the accident'. The report concludes: 'in accordance with our terms of reference, we therefore report that in our opinion blame for the accident is not to be imputed to Captain Thain.'

These findings are at variance with those of two inquiries conducted by the Germans, which declared that the decisive cause of the accident lay in wing icing and that runway slush was a further cause. The latest inquiry heard 27 witnesses and the commission sat in London, Bremen and Frankfurt. The central witness was Captain Thain who, since the accident, has spent more than £1,000 trying to clear his name. He told the inquiry that before the unsuccessful take-off he and his co-pilot looked out of the windows and the wings looked clean. The Fay commission examined a photograph produced by the German investigators. It was taken from the airport building just before the Elizabethan's departure. The photograph appeared to show some snow on the wings. After examining an enlargement of the original negative, the Joint Air Reconnaissance Intelligence Centre decided that the whiteness on the wings may have been light reflected from the wet surface, and not ice as previously thought.

PICTURE ACKNOWLEDGEMENTS

FIRST PLATE SECTION
1. Coloursport
2a Hulton Deutsch Collection
2b Coloursport
3a Coloursport
3b Topham Picture Source
4a Hulton Deutsch Collection
4b Associated Press Agency
5 Associated Press Agency
6a Topham Picture Source
6b Associated Press Agency
7 Coloursport
8a Coloursport

SECOND PLATE SECTION
1a Topham Picture Source
1b Topham Picture Source
2a Coloursport
2b Associated Press Agency
3 Hulton Deutsch Collection
4a Hulton Deutsch Collection
4b Syndication International
5a Topham Picture Source
5b Topham Picture Source
6 Hulton Deutsch Collection
7a Syndication International
7b Syndication International
7c Syndication International
8 Coloursport

Jacket: Hulton Deutsch Collection